# HER
# STORY
# WOMEN
# FROM
# CANADA'S
# PAST

# HER STORY

## WOMEN FROM CANADA'S PAST

Susan E Merritt

**Vanwell Publishing Limited**
St. Catharines, Ontario

To Catherine and Blake

**Canadian Cataloguing in Publication Data**

Merritt, Susan E.
    Her story : women from Canada's past

Includes bibliographical references and index.
ISBN 1-55125-000-4

1.   Women - Canada - Biography - Juvenile literature.
2.   Women - Canada - History - Juvenile literature.
3.   Indians of North America - Canada - Women -
Biography - Juvenile literature. 4. Women, Black -
Canada - Biography - Juvenile literature. 5. Women
immigrants - Canada - Biography - Juvenile literature.
6.   Europeans - Canada- Biography - Juvenile
literature. I. Title.

FC26.W6M4 1993        j305.4'092'271        C93-094639-1
F1005.M4 1993

Design Susan Nicholson
Maps Loris Gasparotto

Vanwell Publishing Limited
1 Northrup Crescent
P.O. Box 2131
St. Catharines, Ontario  L2M 6P5

Printed in Canada
98 97 96 95 94        10 9 8 7 6 5 4 3

Cover: Detail of *Yesterday-Today* AN 56-05-12-139
Copyright© Canadian War Museum
Canadian Museum of Civilization
Photos for CWM by William Kent

# CONTENTS

# INTRODUCTION

Her Story is a celebration of the courage, strength and determination of women. Women make up over half the population of Canada, yet their experiences have often been left out of Canadian history books. Readers were left to wonder about the lives of women in the place we now call Canada. What were their joys and sorrows? What adventures did women have? What events changed their lives? How did women change the world around them?

Her Story is a celebration of the richness and variety of women's lives in Canada's past. Marie de la Tour was a wealthy woman, but Mary Shadd Cary struggled with poverty. Pauline Johnson lived in Canada all her life, but Flora Macdonald stayed only a few years. Dr. Emily Stowe set a goal and worked hard to reach it, but Laura Secord was forced into her ordeal. Madeleine Jarret Tarieu became a hero at age fourteen, but Emily Carr was largely ignored until she reached the age of seventy.

The stories of these sixteen women—native women, black women and European women, all born before 1900—celebrate who we were and who we are. Some are stories of sorrow. Lucy Maud Montgomery was secretly unhappy and ill from the strain of being a perfect wife. Molly Brant agonized over the fate of the First Nations in North America. Shawnadithit, as the last of her race, outlived every person she knew and loved.

Many are stories of triumph. Thanadelthur brought peace to her people. Harriet Tubman Davis led other slaves to freedom. Martha Black tossed aside a life of ease and thrived in the rollicking frenzy of a gold rush town. Emily Murphy and Nellie McClung, both "proper" ladies, ignored society's rules of "hear no evil, see no evil" and worked tirelessly to change laws and improve women's lives.

Women did not meekly sit beside their spinning wheels or cooking fires. They became leaders, doctors, artists and award-winning writers; women defended forts, began newspapers, passed on military secrets and rescued princes. Their stories should not be ignored or forgotten.

So come and celebrate Canada's exciting history; come and read about sixteen women from Canada's past.

ARCTIC OCEAN

PACIFIC OCEAN

Dawson

Yukon

Northwest Territories

British Columbia

Alberta

Saskatchewan

Edmonton

York Factory

Manitoba

Prince Albert

Vancouver

Victoria

Manitou

Winnipeg

Ontario

Quebec

Quebec City

Montreal

Verchères

Fort La Tour

Port-Royal

Cavendish

P.E.I.

Charlottetown

N.B.

N.S.

Windsor

Halifax

St. Joh

Nfld.

ATLANTIC OCEAN

Toronto

U. S. A.

0        500 km

see enlargement

Lake Huron

Leaskdale

Norval

Toronto

Cataraqui

Lake Ontario

Queenston

St. Catharines

Brantford

Chatham

Windsor

Lake Erie

# CHAPTER 1

## MUSKETEER IN PETTICOATS

# MARIE JACQUELIN DE LA TOUR

## (1602 - 1645)

**The most remarkable woman in Acadia's early history**

*Marie stood on the ramparts of Fort La Tour, glaring at the enemy ships anchored out in the channel. They're big, fat spiders, she thought bitterly, ready to devour us like a fly.*

*And La Tour? Where was her husband, she wondered. Why hadn't he returned with ships and soldiers and supplies?*

*The fort's sentry gave a sudden cry of alarm. Marie felt her mouth go dry as she watched the enemy ships sail toward them on the rising tide.*

*The last, desperate battle had begun.*

## MARRIAGE TO A STRANGER

Françoise-Marie Jacquelin was born in France in 1602. Little is known about Marie's early life except that she was possibly a member of the French nobility. In 1640, Marie Jaquelin accepted a marriage proposal from a man named Charles de Saint-Etienne de La Tour. La Tour, who was then living in Acadia, had sent a scout back to France to find a healthy and wealthy woman to be his wife.

Marie Jaquelin accepted La Tour's marriage offer and sailed off into the unknown to marry a man she had probably never met. Marie, however, quickly became La Tour's loyal and courageous partner in his bitter feud over the control of Acadia. It was a feud that would lead to Marie's death.

## ACADIA

Acadia, an area that is now New Brunswick, Nova Scotia and Prince Edward Island, lay between the English colonies to the south and the French colonies to the north and west. The French and British had often feuded over the ownership of this rich land. However in 1640, when

**Photograph of a Micmac child. Charles de la Tour lived with the Micmacs for ten years, married a Micmac woman and had three children.**

Marie arrived to marry La Tour, it was La Tour and another Frenchman who fought over the control of Acadia.

## A FRENCH CIVIL WAR

La Tour had arrived in Acadia in 1610 with a small group of French fur traders. He was fourteen at the time. The fur traders roamed about Acadia and became friends with the Micmacs, one of the First Nations who lived in the area. La Tour eventually married a Micmac woman.

In the 1630s the war with Britain ended and French settlers, later known as Acadians, arrived to begin a new life in Acadia. King Louis

**The rivers and forests of New Brunswick teemed with life. The flocks of birds were so huge that sometimes they blocked out the sun.**

XIII, the King of France, however, made a number of confusing announcements. La Tour and a man by the name of Charles de Menou d'Aulnay were each, separately, placed in charge of Acadia.

D'Aulnay, who lived at Port-Royal (now Annapolis Royal, Nova Scotia) was not a man who could share power. He claimed control over all of Acadia for himself, and was determined to drive out La Tour.

La Tour, who believed strongly in his own right to control Acadia, was equally determined to defend his right—with violence, if necessary. He built his own fort, Fort La Tour, at the mouth of the Saint John River, on the edge of what is now the city of Saint John, New Brunswick. The rival forts were separated only by the Bay of Fundy.

Both men completely ignored the land rights of the Micmacs. When Marie arrived in Acadia, the two quarrelsome French leaders  soon began the violent struggle that would continue for the rest of Marie's life.

## FORT LA TOUR

La Tour's official title was lieutenant governor of Acadia.  His home, however, was only a clump of plain, wooden buildings inside a fence made from upright logs. Compared to Marie's home in France, Fort La Tour must have been a rough and uncomfortable place for Marie to live. The simple buildings, however, contained fine pottery, glass and other elegant and expensive items. These items were probably brought by Marie to furnish her new home.

The early Europeans were afraid of the dark forests, which covered

**11**

**The spectacular Reversing Falls on the Saint John River amazed all who saw it. The inhabitants of Fort La Tour could hear the roar of the Reversing Falls grow suddenly quiet when the powerful sea tide forced the river to change direction. Shown above is a view of the falls painted in 1805—150 years after Marie's battle to save the fort.**

the land. The honking of wild geese in the sky overhead, the beavers hammering mud into their dams with their tails, the thud and splash of salmon leaping in shallow water—these strange, night noises were sometimes loud enough to wake the Europeans who slept inside the tiny fort.

The land was rich and there was plenty of fish and game to catch. Items, however, such as wheat flour, guns and ammunition, had to be imported from France.

## HOME TO FRANCE

D'Aulnay sent letters to the French king, complaining bitterly about La Tour. D'Aulnay's father had some influence at the French court and the King commanded that La Tour turn his fort over to d'Aulnay and return to France as d'Aulnay's prisoner to explain his actions.

La Tour angrily refused and d'Aulnay blockaded Fort La Tour with his ships. Supplies or people were now unable to openly move in or out of the fort.

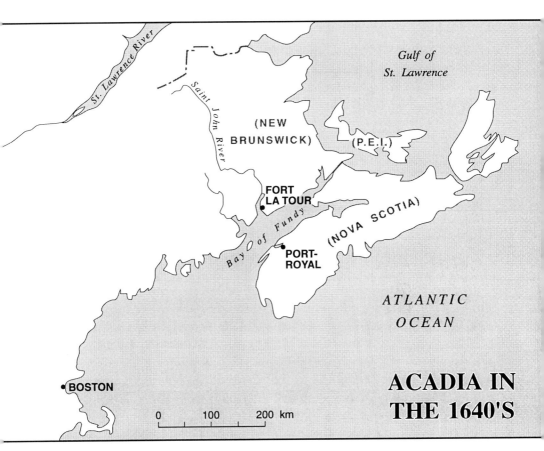

Fort La Tour and Port-Royal faced each other across the Bay of Fundy.

One night La Tour and Marie slipped past d'Aulnay's ships in a row boat and climbed aboard one of La Tour's supply ships that had just arrived from France. Britain and France were no longer at war, so La Tour sailed down the coast to Boston which was part of the British colonies. There Marie and La Tour obtained supplies and four ships and sailed back to Acadia. They chased d'Aulnay's ships back across the Bay of Fundy and blockaded Port-Royal. In the fighting that took place, La Tour killed three of d'Aulnay's men.

Marie knew that d'Aulnay would report the three deaths to the French king and that La Tour would need someone who could explain and defend his actions to the French court. If La Tour himself returned to France, however, d'Aulnay would attack and destroy Fort La Tour. Marie decided she must go on her husband's behalf. She left her husband

13

and her baby son behind and sailed to France to plead her husband's case.

At the French court, Marie discovered d'Aulnay had claimed that La Tour had become partners with the British in order to drive the French out of Acadia. This was not true, but Marie was unable to convince the French court that La Tour was not a traitor. La Tour was found guilty and Marie was forbidden, upon pain of death, to leave France or to send her husband help.

Marie ignored the order, and sent a warning back to La Tour before slipping out of France. She escaped to England and hired an English ship to carry her back to Acadia. The ship took six months to cross the Atlantic because its commander, Captain Bailey, stopped to fish and trade, rather than take her directly to Acadia as he had promised.

When the ship at last headed for Acadia, it was stopped by one of d'Aulnay's ships that was on the lookout for Marie. Marie quickly instructed Captain Bailey to claim the ship was on its way to the English colonies, while she kept out of sight below the decks.

D'Aulnay's men were fooled and let Marie's ship pass. Captain Bailey, however, refused to stop and let Marie off at Fort La Tour. Instead, he sailed his ship directly to Boston. In Boston, an enraged Marie promptly sued the captain for breaking his contract. After a four day trial she was awarded a large sum of money by the court. When Captain Bailey refused to pay, she had the captain arrested and thrown in jail.

Marie then hired three English ships and returned, at last, to Fort La Tour.

## TROUBLE AT FORT LA TOUR

Marie's reunion with her husband and son in December of 1646 must have been a joyful one. Marie, however, quickly discovered Fort La Tour was in deep trouble. D'Aulnay's blockade had stopped all trade and the fort desperately needed supplies. La Tour immediately set sail for Boston leaving Marie in charge of the fort. He planned to buy supplies and return before d'Aulnay discovered he had left Fort La Tour.

Disaster struck after La Tour's departure. Eight of La Tour's men left to join d'Aulnay in Port-Royal. The deserters carried the news to d'Aulnay that La Tour was no longer at the fort.

With food and ammunition low, Marie grew more uneasy with each passing month. Would more men desert? Would d'Aulnay attack? Where was her husband? Was he still in Boston? Was he already dead—his ship

One artist's version of Marie's desperate fight to save Fort La Tour. This portrait appeared on the cover of *The Story of Acadia* by James Hannay.

wrecked by a winter gale?

Marie did not know that La Tour had already sent a small boat with supplies back to Acadia, but the boat had been seized by d'Aulnay. The ship had also carried a letter for Marie from La Tour, promising to return in a month. It was a letter that Marie would not live to read.

## THE LAST BATTLE

When d'Aulnay read La Tour's letter to Marie, he decided to attack Fort La Tour before La Tour returned with more soldiers and supplies. On 12 April 1645, d'Aulnay sailed up the channel with two of his ships and attacked Fort La Tour. Marie took command of the fort–a "musketeer in petticoats" as courageous fighting women were sometimes called. Marie and her tiny group of forty-five loyal men successfully defended the fort for three days and three nights.

In the battle, twenty of d'Aulnay's men were killed and thirteen were wounded. D'Aulnay's larger ship was struck and sank upon a sand bar in the bay.

The fourth day was Easter Sunday and d'Aulnay, who was a devout Christian, did not order an attack. D'Aulnay did, however, manage to use Easter Sunday to bribe one of Marie's men who was a hired Swiss soldier. During that soldier's early morning watch the next day, the bribed soldier did not give the alarm when d'Aulnay attacked. Marie awoke to find d'Aulnay's men inside the fort's first set of walls.

She and her loyal men rushed to defend the fort and the two sides fought, in hand-to-hand combat, inside the fort. Finally d'Aulnay called upon Marie to surrender. At first she refused, even though she and her men were exhausted and short of ammunition. When, however, d'Aulnay swore that the lives of all those inside the fort would be saved, Marie reluctantly surrendered. The situation was hopeless for Fort La Tour, but at least, she thought, the lives of her men would be spared.

## BETRAYAL

As soon as d'Aulnay took possession of Fort La Tour, he went back on his word. Instead of sparing Marie's men, d'Aulnay hanged all but two. Only the Swiss soldier and another soldier who agreed to act as the hangman, were spared. Wearing a rope around her own neck, Marie was forced to watch the execution of her loyal supporters.

Marie became d'Aulnay's prisoner. She secretly wrote a letter of warning to La Tour that she hoped to pass on to the sympathetic Micmacs. The letter, however, was discovered.

Marie died in prison, three weeks after the execution of her men. Some claim Marie died of a broken heart. Some claim she was poisoned by d'Aulnay. No one knows what happened to Marie's young son.

## LA TOUR

La Tour heard about the taking of Fort La Tour and hid in Quebec until his enemy Charles d'Aulnay drowned a few years later in the Bay of Fundy. La Tour then returned to France and presented his side of the story. The French court listened to what he had to say and then again named La Tour lieutenant governor of Acadia.

La Tour returned to Acadia and married for a third time. This time he married the widow of his old enemy, Charles d'Aulnay. La Tour, his third wife and their children lived at Fort La Tour until La Tour's death in 1666.

As for Marie Jaquelin de La Tour—the first European woman to make a home in the province of New Brunswick—she is remembered today as a woman of courage and spirit.

Further Suggested Reading:

Innis, Mary Quayle, ed. *The Clear Spirit*. Toronto: University of Toronto Press, 1966.

# CHAPTER 2

## WOMAN OF PEACE

# THANADELTHUR

## —————— (1697 - 1717) ——————

**She was ... a Very high spirit and of the Firmest Resolution .**
**—Governor James Knight**

*As the Chipewyan camp came into sight, the young woman's heart raced with joy. Thanadelthur had not seen or heard from her people in over two years. Was her mother still alive? And her brother? What about her friends?*

*Her heart sank a little, however, at the thought of the task that lay ahead. The Chipewyans would be pleased with the gifts she brought from the Hudson's Bay Company. They would not, however, be pleased with what she had to say. She knew the Chipewyans would not want to make peace with the Cree—not after the recent murders.*

*Thanadelthur, however, could not rest until she brought peace to her people.*

## SLAVE WOMAN

Thanadelthur was a member of the Chipewyan nation, one of the First Nations. In the late 1600s and early 1700s the Chipewyans lived in the area that today spreads across northern Saskatchewan and up into the Northwest Territories. Their neighbours to the north were the Caribou Inuit. To the south and east of the Chipewyans lived their traditional enemies, the Cree.

In the spring of 1713, when Thanadelthur was probably in her teens, the Crees attacked a party of Chipewyans. Thanadelthur and other Chipewyan women were captured and taken away as slaves of war.

Both the Chipewyan and Cree nations lived in a rugged land with a harsh northern climate. Survival for these people depended upon the skilled labour of strong women who spent most of their waking hours at work.

In the northern nations, the women turned raw animal skins into leather for clothing, made the clothes and moccasins, netted snowshoes, fetched water, wove the fishing nets, collected berries and fire wood, put

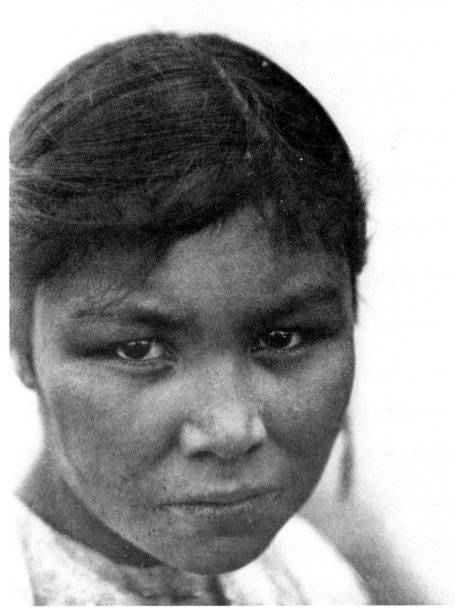

**The First Women: Cree**

up the tents, preserved meat and fish, and prepared the meals.

Native women were valued for their skilled work, rather than just for their appearance. A woman with a lovely face but poor work skills could not keep her family from starvation. Women captured in battle were, therefore, highly prized for the skilled work they could perform as slaves for their new masters.

## ESCAPE

Thanadelthur was a slave for a year and a half before escaping from the Cree with another Chipewyan woman. The two women began to search for their own people, but the task was a difficult one. The Chipewyans were nomadic people who did not live in permanent villages but moved from place to place. During the autumn of 1714 the two women lived on the animals they caught in their own snares as they travelled toward Chipewyan territory.

As winter weather set in, however, the cold and hungry women changed their plan of escape. As slaves, they had seen traders from the Hudson's Bay Company at the Cree camps and they had heard about York Factory, a Hudson's Bay trading post. The women decided to travel through enemy Cree territory and seek shelter at the trading post located at the mouth of the Hayes River.

The trip was a difficult one and along the way the other Chipewyan woman died. Starving and alone, Thanadelthur came across the tracks of a Hudson's Bay hunting party. She followed the tracks back to the hunters' tent and arrived with the hunters at York Factory on 24 November 1714.

## HUDSON'S BAY COMPANY AND THE FUR TRADE

By the late 1500s the hat makers of Europe had created a fashion  that was both stylish and practical—the beaver hat. Hats made with beaver felt were strong and waterproof and could be made in a variety of designs.  As a result, for the next 250 years Europeans were willing to pay high prices for beaver pelts. Europeans also wanted to harvest other types of fur from North America for they had already largely destroyed the fur-bearing wildlife of their own lands.

In 1670 the Hudson's Bay Company was created to provide Europeans with furs supplied by the native trappers and hunters of North America. The company set up trading posts such as York Factory along the shores of Hudson's Bay and waited for the native people to bring their furs to trade. The company did not try to conquer their native

**The First Women: Chipewyan women on a duck hunt**

trading partners, take their land or change their beliefs or religion.
European peddler and native trapper met on an almost equal footing—
each one eager for what the other had to offer.

Before the arrival of the Europeans, the Cree had traded furs to the
Huron people in exchange for corn. Once the European trade began, the
Cree quickly became major suppliers in the European fur trade business.
Cree hunters traded furs for many things, including guns that they used
in their war against their traditional enemies, the Chipewyans.

## A PROBLEM FOR JAMES KNIGHT

James Knight, the Hudson's Bay Company governor of York Factory,
had heard about the Chipewyan people and was eager to trade with them.
The Chipewyans, however, did not have guns and were unwilling to
travel across enemy Cree territory to the Hudson's Bay trading post.

Knight decided the Chipewyans would come to Hudson's Bay

trading posts only if the Cree and Chipewyan were at peace. The Hudson's Bay Company wanted to begin peace talks. However, Cree, Chipewyan and English were all different languages. Knight first had to find an interpreter who could speak all three.

## A SOLUTION FOR JAMES KNIGHT

Knight was delighted when Thanadelthur, a Chipewyan who had lived with the Cree, arrived at York Factory in the winter of 1714. Thanadelthur learned English at York Factory and spoke with enthusiasm about her people and their plentiful supply of furs. Knight listened to the words of the

**The First Women: Inuit**

attractive, energetic woman and became even more determined to begin trade with the Chipewyans.

He convinced the Cree who lived along the Hayes River to send an expedition into Chipewyan territory on a mission of peace. On 27 June 1715, approximately 150 people, including Thanadelthur and a Hudson's Bay employee by the name of William Stuart, left York Factory to find the Chipewyans and begin peace talks. Thanadelthur also carried the message that the Hudson's Bay Company planned to establish another trading post called Churchill at the mouth of the Churchill River.

## NATIVE WOMEN AND THE FUR TRADE

Thanadelthur knew the peace expedition across "The Barren Lands" of the North would be long and dangerous. Why, then, did she risk her life to help the Hudson's Bay Company? It may be that Thanadelthur hated the war between the Chipewyan and Cree people—a war that killed friends and relatives and had once made her a slave. It may also be that she quickly realized the difference many European trade goods would make in the life of overworked native women.

Before the arrival of European trade goods, native women had to use a tremendous amount of skill and energy just to heat water. First they gathered spruce roots and birch bark. Then they made thread out of the spruce roots and sewed birch bark pieces together to create watertight containers. Finally, the birch bark containers were filled with water and hot rocks were dropped in to heat the water.

Trade with Europeans, however, meant the arrival of metal kettles that could be placed directly over a fire.

**The First Women: Kootenay**

Not only was it easier to heat water, but women soon discovered they could use the metal kettles to prepare soups and stews. As well, the arrival of European woolen and cotton goods for tents and clothing meant women no longer had to spend as many hours tanning raw animal skins to create leather.

Native women could directly take part in the fur trade for it was their job to snare and trap birds and small fur-bearing animals such as hare, marten and mink. The animals the women snared belonged to them and the women could trade their pelts to the Hudson's Bay Company for the trade goods of their choice. No doubt they bought items that lessened their own heavy work load.

It is not surprising, therefore, that Thanadelthur did all she could to encourage the fur trade between the Hudson's Bay Company and her own people.

## DISASTER ALONG THE WAY

Food was scarce during the long journey through the Barren Lands and the members of the peace mission suffered from illness and starvation. Eventually most of the men gave up and turned back. Thanadelthur, William Stuart, and about a dozen Cree, however, pressed on.

European men thought of women as physically weak, delicate creatures who could not survive without the kindness and protection of men. Chipewyans, however, laughed at the idea that women were the weaker sex. Chipewyan women like Thanadelthur were, from birth, expected to be physically stronger than men. Chipewyans took it for granted that one woman could pull or carry twice as much as any man. In the summer women carried up to 60 kilograms on their backs and in the winter they hauled much greater loads in sleds and toboggans.

Chipewyan women were also expected to survive, when necessary, on very little food. As a Chipewyan chief later explained, when food was scarce, Chipewyan women could stay alive merely by licking their fingers! Thanadelthur was, therefore, able to press on through the Barren Lands when so many men turned back.

The peace mission eventually came across the bodies of nine Chipewyans. They had been recently killed by a group of Cree who had not been a part of the peace mission. Worried about Chipewyan revenge, the Cree members of the party wanted to turn back at once. Thanadelthur, however, did not agree.

## THANADELTHUR TAKES CONTROL

Unwilling to give up the mission to find her people, Thanadelthur persuaded William Stuart and the Cree to set up camp for ten days. In the meantime, she would travel on alone, find her people and bring them back for peace talks. Thanadelthur seized the chance to become more than an interpreter. Her bold plan made her the dominating force of the peace mission.

Alone, Thanadelthur followed the tracks of the Chipewyans until, a few days later, she found her own people. A large group of them had gathered to plan revenge against the Cree for the killing of the nine Chipewyans.

She rejoiced to be back with her people but knew she had a difficult job ahead of her. She had to convince a group who had gathered for revenge, to forget the recent murders and seek peace instead. Chipewyan women were, however, consulted about important matters and they influenced the decisions. Thanadelthur knew, therefore, that her arguments would receive close attention.

Thanadelthur talked to the Chipewyans until she was hoarse, trying to persuade them to make peace with their traditional enemies. She was a forceful woman, but it still took all her persuasive powers to convince her people of the wisdom of peace.

In the end she was successful and Thanadelthur triumphantly returned to the camp of William Stuart and the Cree peace mission with over one hundred Chipewyans. She returned, as promised, ten days after she had left the Cree camp.

During the peace talks that followed Thanadelthur sat on a raised platform so that she could easily be seen. William Stuart later reported that during the peace talks she argued with some and pressured others until she forced them all to agree to peace.

The peace expedition returned to York Factory where Thanadelthur, accompanied by ten other Chipewyans, spent the winter of 1716-1717. There she took a husband—probably one of the Chipewyan men who had come back with her to the trading post.

## A WOMAN OF POWER

William Stuart freely admitted that the peace expedition owed its success to the remarkable Thanadelthur. Her role in the peace mission earned for her the respect of native and European alike.

For the Chipewyans, she was their only link with the European peddlers and their important trade goods. Her advice was often sought on fur trade matters.

For Governor James Knight, she was a valuable source of advice and information. Knight often asked Thanadelthur for her opinion about his plans for the new trading post. She also spoke of rich copper deposits to the north and of other native people who owned "yellow metal." Knight believed the yellow metal was gold and became even more eager to establish the Hudson's Bay post of Churchill.

## PLANS FOR ANOTHER EXPEDITION

As soon as the winter passed, Knight planned to send Thanadelthur and the Chipewyans at York Factory out on another expedition. They were to spread the word to all Chipewyans that Churchill would be built that summer.

Thanadelthur was enthusiastic about the idea and was willing to leave her husband behind if he did not want to make the long journey. She

## The First Women: Haida

planned to personally contact all Chipewyans with the news—a strenuous journey that would take about two and a half years to complete.

The Chipewyans at York Factory would not have considered it unusual for a woman to make such a long journey. Chipewyan men would not travel any great distances without women being included in the party. They knew women were necessary to make and mend clothing and moccasins and snowshoes, paddle canoes, pitch camp, collect food and make the meals along the way.

Samuel Hearne, a European explorer, later learned about the key role of native women the hard way. Hearne's first two attempts to reach the Coppermine River ended in failure because he did not include native women on the expeditions. On his third attempt, however, at the insistence of his Chipewyan guide, Chipewyan women who had been chosen for their strength and skill became an important part of the expedition. With their assistance, Hearne's third expedition in 1771 was a success.

## DISEASE AND DEATH

When Europeans first arrived in North America they were astonished at the general healthiness of the native population. By comparison, the Europeans were scrawny, malnourished and diseased. In 1624, one amazed European wrote that among the people of the First Nations "there are few or none cross-eyed, blind, crippled, lame, hunchbacked or limping men; all are well-fashioned people, strong and sound of body, well fed, without blemish."

One northern native woman later spoke with contempt about the bandy legs, humpbacks and other deformities of so many of the Europeans who visited her land.

The excellent health of the native people of North America, however, immediately changed after they made contact with the Europeans and their plagues. Although the First Nations of North America were often as different from each other as Scots were from Spaniards, all were ravaged by the terrible diseases from Europe.

Before Thanadelthur could leave York Factory on the next expedition, she became ill. In his journal, Knight suggests that she suffered from a change in her normal lifestyle and from a lack of fresh food. It is, however, more likely that Thanadelthur caught one of the European diseases that killed so many native people.

Governor Knight did all that he could to make her well, but Thanadelthur, the woman who had been his interpreter, guide, consultant and peace negotiator, died on 5 February 1717. Knight, grief-stricken at the death of this intelligent and courageous woman, wrote "I am almost ready to break my heart."

Thanadelthur, the remarkable woman who had once been a slave, brought peace to her people and became a part of fur trade history.

Further Suggested Reading:

Van Kirk, Sylvia. *Many Tender Ties*. Winnipeg: Watson & Dwyer Publishing Ltd., 1986.

# CHAPTER 3

## HERO OF VERCHÈRES

# MADELEINE JARRET TARIEU

## (1678 - 1747)

**Allow me to tell you that I sometimes aspire to fame quite as eagerly as many men.**

—**Madeleine Jarret Tarieu**

*Madeleine raced toward Fort Verchères with an Iroquois warrior in pursuit. As she raced along, Madeleine's scarf fluttered about her neck.*

*Would she reach the fort's wooden gate in time? Once inside, she would be safe. If she did not reach Fort Verchères, however, she would be killed or taken prisoner.*

*Heart pounding, Madeleine put on a burst of speed as the warrior, now directly behind her, reached out and grabbed her scarf. Madeleine screamed with terror and clutched at her throat.*

## THE WARS BEGIN

From the early 1500s, the Iroquois and the Hurons, two powerful First Nations, traded with European fishermen and fur traders for valuable items such as cloth, iron axes and metal pots. Each nation believed that control of this important trade was necessary for its own survival. Bloody wars were fought to decide which rival First Nation would control the fur trade with the Europeans.

The Iroquois, also called the Six Nations, were a farming and trading society of about thirty thousand people who lived, for the most part, south of the St Lawrence River.

The Hurons, a farming and trading society of about twenty thousand people, were bitter enemies of the Iroquois. The Erie, Neutral, Petun, Algonquins and Montagnais nations, however, were all friends and allies of the Huron nation. The Hurons and their allies lived north of the St Lawrence River and the Great Lakes.

Samuel de Champlain, a French explorer, set up the French colony of

**A Montagnais Lodge. The Montagnais were early trading partners of the French.**

New France along the St Lawrence River in 1608. The Hurons were the trading partners of the French. In order to show support for his trading partners, Champlain joined the Hurons and their allies and attacked the Iroquois in 1609. From then on, the French and Iroquois were bitter enemies.

## THE CARIGAN REGIMENT

Although there were short periods of peace, the wars between the Iroquois and the French lasted almost one hundred years. Each side killed enemy men, women and children, and each side attacked enemy villages and burned each other's crops and buildings.

From 1660 to 1665 Iroquois attacks terrorized the French colony and over two hundred settlers were killed. In 1665, France sent over one thousand soldiers, known as the Carigan Regiment, (Régiment de Carigan) to defend the colony.

The Iroquois made peace with the French in 1667, for they too were suffering. Like many First Nations, thousands of Iroquois were dying from the terrible diseases that Europeans had brought to North America– diseases such as measles and smallpox. As well, the Iroquois had lost many of their people in the ongoing wars.

A regiment of French soldiers was no longer needed and the Carigan Regiment was broken up. One of the soldiers in the Carigan Regiment was young François Jarret, a nephew of the regiment's commander. Jarret, like many of the men in the regiment, decided to stay in New France, and in 1669 he married twelve-year-old Marie Perrot. The fourth child of Marie and François Jarret would one day become famous as the courageous Madeleine of Verchères.

## THE SEIGNEURY OF VERCHÈRES

New France adopted the system of land grants used in France and much of Europe. The King of France saw himself as the owner of New France and he rewarded certain people by giving them large sections of land in the colony. The landowner was called a seigneur and the land a seigneury.

**The farm fields lay outside the stockade of Fort Verchères. Above, an early French farmer plants his crops around the tree stumps.**

The seigneurs rented much of their land out to families who did not have any land. These families farmed the land and gave some of their farm crops to their seigneur as rent. The farm families were called habitants.

As a reward for his work as a soldier in the Carigan Regiment, Madeleine's father was given a large seigneury on the St Lawrence River that he called Verchères. Madeleine was born in Verchères six years later, the fourth of twelve children.

During the years when New France was at peace, the settlers concentrated on clearing the land and planting crops such as barley, wheat and oats. Like the Iroquois and Hurons, the French settlers also planted corn. Each family worked hard to grow and harvest enough food to get them through the long winter months.

## A RICH LAND

Settlers could also hunt, fish and gather food in a land bursting with life. Strawberries, currants, cherries, raspberries, blueberries and blackberries grew wild in the forests. The St Lawrence River, as clear and clean as pure spring water, was full of smelt, shad, mackerel, salmon, herring and cod. It was also home to walruses, seals, porpoises, whales, beaver, otter and muskrats. Elk, deer, moose and caribou and bear roamed freely in the forests. Some river islands were so thick with ducks, geese and Canada geese that the grass could not be seen.

In France, firewood was scarce and every stick of wood was expensive. In New France, however, wood was cheap and plentiful—even the poorest family could have a blazing fire on cold winter nights.

Madeleine's father taught his children how to load and fire a musket. It took months to learn how to properly use a musket. Madeleine was an excellent shot and often went hunting with her family. Her talent with a musket was soon put to another use.

## CHATEAU DANGEREUX

By 1681, the Iroquois, feeling more and more cut off from the fur trade, again began to attack New France. In 1689, France and England declared war against each other. The Iroquois were encouraged by the English, their allies and trading partners, to continue their attacks against the French.

As the seigneur of Verchères, the first duty of Madeleine's father was to protect the habitants and his family. He built a fort to protect his family and his habitants in case of Iroquois attack. The fort was a rough,

**The Falls of St Feriole, Quebec. The forests and rivers of New France were full of wildlife. On one island, a single musket shot could kill two to three hundred birds.**

wooden wall over five metres high (a stockade) in a rectangular shape around the seigneur's house and other buildings. Madeleine's home at Verchères now became Fort Verchères.

The Iroquois war parties often traveled north to New France along the Richelieu River. Fort Verchères was, unfortunately, located near the Richelieu River. As well, if the Iroquois did attack the fort, it would take at least one day for soldiers to arrive from the French settlement of Montreal. As a result, Fort Verchères was known as *Chateau Dangereux* or Dangerous Castle.

## THE FIRST HERO OF VERCHÈRES

In 1690, the Iroquois attacked Fort Verchères by trying to climb over the stockade. Madeleine's mother, Marie, had only her children and three or four men with her at the time of the attack. Marie, who was thirty-three at the time, took command of the fort and forced the Iroquois back several times with musket fire. Fort Verchères remained under attack for two days until Marie and her tiny group forced the Iroquois to leave shortly before help arrived from Montreal.

Twelve-year-old Madeleine, who was in Fort Verchères at the time, probably helped by carrying ammunition and by keeping her younger brothers and sisters out of sight. She must have watched and learned a great deal from her mother's strength and courage.

An etching of Quebec, 1683. Madeleine's father was in Quebec when the 1692 attack on Fort Verchères took place.

## IN COMMAND

After 1690, the French settlers of New France went on the attack and swept down into the English colonies of New York and New England. Using the same tactics the Iroquois used against them, the French attacked small English towns and outposts, killed, burned and then fled with prisoners before their surprised enemies could fight back.

The fighting continued back and forth. In 1691 the Iroquois attacked New France and killed more than one hundred settlers. Madeleine's sixteen-year-old brother and her two brothers-in-law were killed by Iroquois.

In 1692, Fort Verchères was well supplied with muskets and gun powder, but the summer passed without attack. In October, Madeleine's father left by boat to look after business in Quebec while Madeleine's mother traveled to Montreal to buy supplies for the upcoming winter. Madeleine was left in charge of Fort Verchères. An elderly soldier was left behind to guard the fort.

## TO ARMS!

On 22 October 1692 most of the habitants were out working in the fields when forty or fifty Iroquois attacked. The Iroquois quickly captured approximately twenty settlers who had been working out in the fields. Madeleine, who was working in a vegetable garden two hundred paces outside the stockade at the time, turned and ran toward the gate of Fort Verchères. An Iroquois warrior quickly overtook Madeleine and grabbed her by her scarf. Madeleine tore off the scarf and escaped by leaving it behind. She rushed through the gate, slammed it shut and sounded the alarm. "To arms! To arms!" she shouted.

Inside the fort, some of the women wept for their husbands who had been captured by the Iroquois. Madeleine, however, had no time for sorrow and despair. The others in the fort—mostly women and children—were depending on her as their leader.

She quickly climbed on the stockades beside the only soldier in the fort and took command. Madeleine put on a soldier's hat and gestured and shouted loudly. She hoped the Iroquois would think the fort was full of soldiers and therefore difficult to attack and destroy. Madeleine quickly fired off a small cannon to warn the other small French forts along the St Lawrence and to signal for help. She knew the other forts would hear the sound of the cannon and pass along the message to the soldiers at Montreal that Fort Verchères was under attack.

The Iroquois now surrounded the fort and Madeleine knew it would be a full day before help would arrive from Montreal. She did not dare take time to eat or sleep.

When it grew dark, those inside the fort watched and waited. Would there be more Iroquois attacks? The Iroquois preferred surprise attacks because their own warriors were less likely to be killed. Madeleine knew the Iroquois might use a clever trick to slip into the fort and launch another surprise attack. She was cautious, therefore, when the fort's cattle gathered in the dark outside the gate, lowing to come inside. Madeleine wondered if there were there Iroquois covered with cattle skins hiding among the cattle.

The next day the Iroquois slipped back into the dense forests and about an hour later help arrived from Montreal—one hundred French soldiers by boat and fifty native allies by land.

Fourteen-year-old Madeleine greeted the French lieutenant as a soldier would, by saying "Monsier, I surrender my arms to you."

The native allies, probably Algonquin or Montagnais, caught up with the Iroquois war party on Lake Champlain, freed the captive French settlers and brought them back to Fort Verchères.

## MADELEINE TELLS HER STORY

After the French and English made peace in 1697, the seigneury at Fort Verchères had trouble surviving. In 1699, Madeleine wrote to the Comtesse de Maurepas in France and told her about the Iroquois attack on Verchères. Madeleine hoped to receive a reward for her bravery which would help her father with the seigneury. The members of the

MADELEINE de VERCHÈRES · 1678 · 1747

BORN at Sorel, in the Province of Quebec, 1678, Madeleine de Verchères is one of Canada's National heroines. On October 22nd 1692, at the age of fourteen and a half years, she, with the help of her two brothers, aged twelve and ten years, successfully defended FORT DE VERCHÈRES against attack by 45 Iroquois Indians. Madeleine de Verchères symbolizes the feminine heroism of CANADA. Died at Ste-Anne de la Perade, Quebec.

*YESTERDAY*

TO·DAY

**Madeleine is an example of wartime courage in this World War II recruiting poster.**

French court were interested in her story. When Madeleine's father died in 1700, his pension, which he had received as a former member of the Carigan Regiment, was transferred to Madeleine as a reward.

The Iroquois signed a peace treaty with the French in 1701. As in 1667, war and disease were shattering this powerful nation and the Iroquois wanted time to heal.

In 1706, Madeleine married a French lieutenant by the name of Pierre-Thomas Tarieu de la Perade. The couple lived at a seigneury at Sainte-Anne-de-la-Perade and had five children. Madeleine was still an expert with the musket, and it was said there was "no Canadian or officer who was a better musket shot" than Madeleine. In 1722, Madeleine saved her husband's life when he was involved in a fight with two huge men.

Madeleine died at the age of sixty-nine. Today, three hundred years after the battle, the name Madeleine de Verchères remains a Canadian symbol of valour and determination.

Further Suggested Reading:

Grant, Janet. *Madeleine de Verchères*. Toronto: Grolier Limited, 1989.

# CHAPTER 4

## HIGHLAND HERO AND LOYALIST

# FLORA MACDONALD

### —————— (1722 - 1790) ——————

**Flora Macdonald: A name that will be mentioned in history, and if courage and fidelity be virtues, mentioned with honour.**

**—Dr Samuel Johnson**

*Flora watched the island coastline come closer as her men pulled at the oars. In her hand was the all-important travel pass—the pass that gave her group permission to land on the Isle of Skye.*

*She glanced at her maid Betty—an awkward creature who had tripped over her skirts while leaping into the rowboat earlier. Betty caught Flora's eye and gave her mistress a saucy wink.*

*Flora smiled politely then nervously turned again to gaze at the coast of Skye. As their boat approached the island a group of men began to fire at them from the shore.*

*Heart pounding, Flora crouched to avoid the bullets. They had been betrayed, she thought frantically.*

## FAIR ONE

Flora Macdonald was born in 1722 in the Hebrides, which is a group of islands along the northwest coast of Scotland that includes the Isle of Skye. Her father died when she was two, and Flora and her brother Angus lived on the Isle of Skye with their mother and Hugh Macdonald, their stepfather.

Flora's first name was really Fionnghal which means "fair one" in Gaelic. This name was later translated into the English name of Flora.

Flora's first language was Gaelic but she was well educated and learned to speak fluent English. She also learned to read and to write in both Gaelic and English and to play the harp.

Flora visited many of the islands of the Hebrides, including the island of Benbecula where some of Flora's relatives lived. It was on Benbecula in 1746 that Flora first met Bonnie Prince Charlie.

# BONNIE PRINCE CHARLIE

For years England's Protestants and Roman Catholics fought, tortured and killed each other over religion and politics. Eventually the Roman Catholic Stuart family was forced off the throne of England and Scotland, and the Protestant Hanover family from Germany became the rulers of the country.

Charles Edward Stuart, the eldest grandson of the last Stuart king, King James II, wanted to put the Stuarts back on the throne of England and Scotland. The Stuarts originally came from Scotland, and Charles Stuart believed there were still many Jacobites (those who supported the Stuart claim to the throne) in Scotland.

Charles, who was charming, brave and handsome, was nicknamed "Bonnie Prince Charlie" by his followers. He arrived in Scotland in 1745 to start a rebellion against King George II, a Hanover, in order to regain the throne. The Scottish clans from the Highlands of Scotland joined the small army of Charles Stuart and managed to win a few battles against King George and his soldiers. Half of Charles' supporters were Roman Catholic, while the rest were Protestant.

## VICTORY FOR STINKING BILLIE

At Culloden, however, on a windswept Scottish moor, Charles Stuart and his Highlanders were defeated by soldiers led by King George's second son, William, Duke of Cumberland. The Duke of Cumberland was a brutal man who ordered the killing of all those in Charles Stuart's army who had been wounded or taken prisoner. As further punishment, the homes of many Highlanders were burned and their cattle taken away.

In England, a flower was named Sweet William in honour of William, the Duke of Cumberland. In Scotland, however, where the Duke was viewed as a ruthless butcher, the same flower was called Stinking Billie. The flower still bears that name in Scotland today.

## BETTY BURKE

Charles Stuart escaped from the Battle of Culloden and went into hiding in Scotland. King George offered a huge reward for the capture of the troublesome Charles Stuart. If captured, Charles would probably be executed for treason.

In June of 1746 Charles, now an outlaw, landed on the island of Benbecula where Flora Macdonald was staying. King George's soldiers also arrived and began to comb the island for Charles Stuart.

The King's soldiers were supposed to be helped by the militia (volunteer soldiers) from the Isle of Skye, but many of those local people secretly supported Bonnie Prince Charlie and his claim to the throne. One of Charles' secret supporters was a captain in the Skye militia—Hugh Macdonald, the stepfather of Flora Macdonald.

Charles had to leave the little island of Benbecula to avoid capture. Nobody, however, was allowed to move about the small island or to leave it without a pass. One of Charles' supporters, possibly Hugh Macdonald, came up with a daring plan to use Flora in Charles' escape.

Flora, with a maid and a man servant, would row across to the Isle of Skye, where her mother lived. Flora often traveled about the islands and this trip would not arouse suspicion. Her own stepfather, Hugh Macdonald, as a captain in the Skye militia, would provide the necessary travel pass for Flora and her servants. It would be an ordinary trip, except that Charles Stuart would be in the boat too. Charles would be disguised as Flora's maid and he would use the name Betty Burke.

## ACROSS THE SEA TO SKYE

Although Flora was a Protestant like her mother, she supported Catholic Charles Stuart and his right to the throne. Flora, now twenty-four, secretly met with Charles and agreed to risk her life to take Charles to the Isle of Skye.

On 28 June 1746 Flora, a man servant, four boatsmen and Charles Stuart, dressed as Betty Burke, rowed across from Benbecula to the Isle of Skye. When they tried to land, the boat was fired upon by suspicious supporters of King George. Flora's group escaped unhurt and landed further north on the island. Flora, with Charles still disguised as Flora's maid, took shelter at several Jacobite homes on Skye.

Charles remained disguised as Betty Burke until 30 June when he changed back into Highland dress. Charles gave Flora a gracious farewell and, with the help of a guide, eventually made his way to France and safety. In spite of the huge reward offered for his capture, the Highlanders never betrayed Charles Stuart.

## A DANCE NAMED AMERICA

Flora was later captured and put in prison on an English troopship for twelve months. She was, however well treated, for even the English viewed her as a hero for her brave role in the escape of Charles Stuart.

In 1750 she married Allan Macdonald who was a supporter of King George and had fought against Charles Stuart's army at the Battle of Culloden. Flora and Allan had seven children and they named their first

THE LOYALISTS
LES LOYALISTES

CANADA

32

**Loyalists came from all classes, professions and religions. Sometimes loyalties divided friends and families. Benjamin Franklin was a famous Patriot but his son, William Franklin, was a Loyalist.**

son Charles—after the "Bonnie Prince."

Allan inherited a large estate, but the Macdonalds had money problems. Violent winter storms, followed by famine, forced the Macdonalds into debt. Life was also difficult in other ways. After the Battle of Culloden, King George punished the Highlanders for their part in the rebellion by trying to destroy the clan system. They were not even allowed to wear tartan or play the bagpipes.

Highlanders began to emigrate to North America hoping to find religious and political freedom in a new home. Some settled in Nova Scotia, some in the Mohawk Valley (on the estate owned by Molly Brant's husband, Sir William Johnson), and some in North Carolina.

Between 1764 and 1776 over twenty-three thousand Highlanders left for America. So many emigrated that one popular dance at Highland parties was named America. The dancers, representing the emigrants, moved around the dance floor in larger and larger circles until they danced right off the dance floor in small groups as if sailing for America. Dr Samuel Johnson, a famous English writer, visited the Macdonalds and was amazed at the large number of Highlanders who were leaving for America.

In 1774 the Macdonalds emigrated to North Carolina, part of the Thirteen Colonies, hoping to improve their finances. They arrived, however, just in time for the outbreak of another rebellion. The American Revolution, another rebellion against another Hanover king, was about to begin.

## LOYALISTS

Those living in the Thirteen Colonies in 1775 had to decide which side to support in the American Revolution. Those who wanted to break away from King George III and British rule, called themselves the Patriots. Those who wanted the Thirteen Colonies to remain under British rule

**A sketch of Windsor, Nova Scotia. Flora's husband was stationed in nearby Halifax.**

called themselves Loyalists. No one was allowed to stay out of the war.

Flora and her husband Allan became active Loyalists. Allan became a captain in the Royal Highland Emigrants. During one clash with the Patriots, it is reported that Flora, by now a fifty-four-year-old grandmother, rode up and down the ranks of Loyalist soldiers shouting words of encouragement.

In 1776 Flora's husband and son were both captured and kept in prison by the Patriots until 1777 when they were traded back to the British for Patriot prisoners. Eventually Allan was sent to his battalion's headquarters in Halifax, Nova Scotia.

## DANGEROUS TIMES

It was dangerous to be a Loyalist in the Thirteen Colonies. Loyalists who refused to swear an oath of allegiance to the new colonial government were outside the protection of the law and could be beaten, robbed, thrown in jail, or even executed. Bands of spiteful Patriots roamed about the country attacking and terrorizing Loyalist homes and families.

Like other Loyalist families, Flora and her daughter and grandsons made their way to New York City, which was under British control. In 1778, Flora moved to Windsor, Nova Scotia, to be near her husband.

Confiscation acts allowed many American states to seize Loyalist property. Driven from their homes, many Loyalists began a new life in Canada, in settlements such as the one above.

Some Loyalists who did not know how to clear the land or even how to farm, struggled to survive in early Canada.

**The Loyalists were Canada's first huge wave of largely European immigrants. Many more immigrants, such as the Scottish family, above, would arrive in the next 250 years.**

## LOYALISTS IN NOVA SCOTIA

Loyalists always feared for their lives when British forces were pulled out of an American city. When the British army left Boston in 1776 and Philadelphia in 1778, thousands of terrified Loyalists left their homes and possessions behind and fled to British territory. As a result, large shiploads of Loyalists began to arrive in Nova Scotia as early as 1776.

The tiny communities of Nova Scotia were soon overrun with Loyalist refugees. The sudden arrival of new inhabitants caused food and housing shortages. Many Loyalists were forced to live in tents until they were given grants of land. Often the land grants Loyalists received were areas of dense forest that they had to clear before they could plant crops.

The largest wave of Loyalist refugees took place in 1783 after Britain lost the war and the peace treaty terms were announced. Loyalists learned that property taken away from them during the American Revolution was not going to be returned. Many decided to begin a new life in another British colony such as the Maritimes, or Upper Canada (now Ontario) or Lower Canada (now Quebec).

## NOT FORGOTTEN

Some British Loyalists returned to live in Great Britain. Flora's health began to fail in Nova Scotia and she returned to the Hebrides in 1780 with her daughter and grandsons. Allan joined her in 1784 and Flora spent her last years on the Macdonald estate on the Isle of Skye. She died suddenly at age sixty-eight, still a Highland hero.

Flora's daring rescue of Charles Stuart has not been forgotten, and today her grave site is a popular tourist attraction on the Isle of Skye.

Further Suggested Reading:

Magee, Joan. *Loyalist Mosaic*. Toronto: Dundurn Press, 1984.

# CHAPTER 5

## LEADER AND LOYAL ALLY

# MOLLY BRANT

## ———— (1736 -1796) ————

**You have great influence with your people, Miss Molly. Your word is law to them.**

**—Colonel John Butler**

*Dark eyes blazing with anger, Molly shook the other woman by the shoulders and demanded, "Where is your husband?"*

*Herkimer's wife gazed in terror at Molly Brant, then dropped her eyes. She tried to break away, but Molly tightened her grip.*

*"Where is your husband? Tell me where Herkimer has gone and why!" If she discovered the location of Nicholas Herkimer's rebel army, Molly could send a Mohawk runner to warn her brother and the others.*

*Molly paused and added in a low voice full of menace "Remember, I am a Clan Mother—do not even think of telling me a lie!"*

*Shaking with fear, Herkimer's wife stammered out all that she knew.*

## EARLY LIFE

Of the many First Nations in North America, the Iroquois or Six Nations are among the most famous. Molly Brant was born in 1736 into the Mohawk nation—one of the leading nations belonging to the Iroquois. Molly's family was an important one–her grandfather had been a *sachem* or peace chief who had traveled to England and visited the King.

Molly grew up in the Mohawk Valley in what is today New York State. The Mohawk people had a great deal of power because they controlled the rich Mohawk Valley which was an important gateway into the centre of North America.

The Mohawks in the Mohawk Valley had grown used to European settlers, and Molly attended a European style school for young ladies. As a result, she grew up able to move with grace and skill in both the Iroquois world and the European world of the new settlers.

The two worlds were very different in their treatment of women.

Iroquois women were considered to be the "Life of the Nation" because of their important role in society. European women, however, were not so fortunate.

## DIFFERENT WORLDS

Iroquois women commanded far greater power and respect in Iroquois communities than European women did among their own people. It was an Iroquois tradition that all Iroquois were descended from the same wise, female ancestor, and therefore all Iroquois women were wise.

The Iroquois were divided into groups called clans with names such as bear or turtle. Iroquois children belonged to their mother's clan and took their mother's clan name. Each clan was led by a powerful Clan Mother. The Clan Mothers chose the peace chief and could get rid of the peace chief if he did not turn out to be a good leader. Clan Mothers also had a voice in the Iroquois councils as advisors and were consulted by chiefs and warriors when there were difficult problems.

In today's terms, it would be as if a select group of women hired and fired the prime minister and sat as a powerful group in Parliament advising the prime minister and the military leaders. In contrast, women European settlers would not even be allowed to vote in elections for another 150 years.

Iroquois women owned and controlled the land as a group and farmed the land together in clan groups, growing many varieties of corn, beans and squash. They also owned the crops, one of the major forms of Iroquois wealth, which the women harvested and preserved. It was the women who decided how the food—even the meat brought back by the hunters—was shared among the villagers so that no one would go hungry.

In the European settler communities, however, the men owned everything—the children, the land, the crops, their wives' wages—even their wives' clothing and jewelry.

Clan Mothers helped to select the group's religious leaders or "keepers of the faith," and half of the religious leaders were women. Iroquois women also had an equal share in organizing and running religious festivals and all other religious matters.

Most European settlers, however, belonged to religions that gave women very little say in the management of their own religions and certainly did not allow women to become religious leaders. Molly herself was a Christian, but she would have been aware of the role women played in the religious traditions of her people.

If Iroquois women disagreed with the decision to wage war, they could prevent the departure of their warriors by refusing to provide the war party with food and moccasins. Iroquois wars were, therefore, impossible without the help and support of the Iroquois women. European women, however, had no formal say in military matters.

## MARRIAGE

Molly's beauty and high social standing caught the attention of Sir William Johnson, the superintendent of Indian Affairs and the most important European settler in the Mohawk Valley. When among the Iroquois, Sir William adopted Mohawk dress and customs and used their language. Time and time again the Iroquois were troubled by greedy Europeans whose only law was the gun. The Iroquois sought Johnson's advice about how to deal with the land-hungry Europeans who broke their promises and stole more and more Iroquois land. Over the years the Mohawks gave their friend Sir William large tracts of their own land as a sign of admiration and respect for the only white man they felt they could trust.

At age twenty-three Molly married Sir William Johnson in an Iroquois ceremony. She did not follow the Iroquois tradition of having her new husband move into her clan's longhouse. Instead, she followed the European custom of moving into her new husband's house—an elegant mansion named Johnson Hall, which is now a museum in Johnstown, New York. There Molly wore fine European clothing and lived the life of a wealthy, upper class European wife. In spite of a busy life running a large household of servants, slaves, employees and six stepchildren from Sir William's two previous marriages, Molly stayed involved in Mohawk life. She kept her birth name for if an Iroquois woman changed her birth name she could not become a Clan Mother.

In her husband's world, Molly was the gracious and capable hostess to her husband's many guests—governors, British lords and peace chiefs. Sir William was often away on long trips, leaving Molly and the servants to run the large and complicated estate and look after her own eight children. As well, important councils held on Sir William's large estates meant Molly was responsible for the feeding of up to nine hundred visitors—for several months at a time!

A few years before the American Revolution Sir William died suddenly leaving Molly a widow at age forty-one. The Iroquois nation deeply mourned the death of their true friend, Sir William Johnson. However another, greater tragedy loomed ahead for Molly and her people. The American Revolution, the war that would shatter the Iroquois nation, was about to begin.

# A DIFFICULT CHOICE

The American Revolution began in 1775 when the Thirteen Colonies refused to be governed by Great Britain any longer. The Iroquois did not want to become involved in a foreigner's war and, at first, kept out of the fighting.

When it soon became obvious that the Iroquois would have to join one side or the other, they faced a difficult decision. Which side should they support? The Thirteen Colonies had grown fat and prosperous by looking the other way when its people stole land from the Iroquois and other native people. If such people won the war, how long, they wondered, could the Iroquois hope to hold on to their remaining land?

The British, on the other hand, knew they would need the superb fighting skills of the Iroquois to put down the American rebellion. They worked hard to win the Iroquois as allies. At the invitation of King George III, Molly's brother Joseph Brant traveled to England. Joseph spoke bluntly to the King about British subjects in the Thirteen Colonies who continued to steal Iroquois land. The King promised stolen Iroquois lands would be returned to the Iroquois after the war. Joseph believed he could trust the word of the British King and decided it would be in the best interests of the Iroquois to become British allies.

Molly agreed. The Iroquois had, after all, successfully fought on the side of the British in earlier wars and she believed that Sir William, had he lived, would have sided with the British. Molly's eldest son, Peter Warren Johnson, became a lieutenant in the British army.

# A NATION TORN APART

The Iroquois held a council and the Mohawk, Onondaga, Cayuga and Seneca nations agreed to become British allies. The warriors chose Joseph Brant to be their war chief. The Oneida and Tuscarora nations, however, decided to support the Thirteen Colonies in the American Revolution.

It was a terrible time of sorrow for the Iroquois as their mighty confederacy–a nation created out of smaller nations—split apart after five hundred years of union. Not only did the confederacy split apart, but Iroquois now fought Iroquois. What began as a war between groups of European foreigners created an Iroquois civil war that caused former friends and relatives to fight each other.

**The First Women: Kalispel**

## THE WARNING

The European settlers also divided over which side to support in the American Revolution. The two Herkimer brothers, both friends and neighbours of Molly and Sir William, split in their support. George Herkimer became a Loyalist and remained loyal to Britain, but his brother Nicholas became a Patriot and a general in the American army.

In the spring of 1777, Nicholas Herkimer marched away at the head of a Patriot army. Molly forced Nicholas Herkimer's Oneida wife to confess that Herkimer was on his way with a Patriot American army to attack Joseph and his warriors outside Fort Stanwix. Molly quickly sent a trusted Mohawk runner to warn her brother Joseph that Herkimer was on the way.

Alerted by Molly, Joseph and his men were able to defeat Herkimer's troops in the Oriskany ravines. Herkimer himself was severely injured and returned to his home, ready to take revenge on Molly Brant for her part in his defeat.

## A TERRIBLE PRICE TO PAY

Many Loyalist settlers had been quickly driven out of the Mohawk Valley by the Patriots. Molly, however, refused to leave and remained in her home guarded by

**The First Women: Quinault**

Mohawk warriors. Soon after Nicholas Herkimer's return, Patriot forces attacked Molly's home by night. The Patriots ransacked Molly's lovely home, stole or destroyed her belongings and threatened her children's lives.

Molly and her children left the Mohawk Valley that night on foot. Penniless and worried about further Patriot attack, Molly and her children hid with her Cayuga relatives. While in hiding, Cayuga and Onondaga chiefs, discouraged by British losses, often sought Molly's advice. Molly always counseled them to remain allies of Britain. Aware of her importance and influence among the Iroquois, Colonel John Butler, who had fought with Joseph Brant when Herkimer was defeated at Oriskany, arranged for Molly and her children to move to Fort Niagara, on Lake Ontario.

## STATESWOMAN AND DIPLOMAT

During the war Molly spent much of her time at Fort Niagara (across the Niagara River from present-day Niagara-on-the Lake, Ontario) and at Fort Haldimand (near present-day Kingston, Ontario). There were large numbers of Iroquois at both forts. Some were families driven out of their own homes by Patriot armies and some were warriors preparing to attack American Patriots.

**The First Women: Sioux**

**The First Women: Tsawatenok**

In spite of her own sorrow—her seventeen-year-old son Peter had been killed while fighting the Patriots—Molly Brant continued to provide counsel and advice to her people. Patriot forces destroyed the huge Seneca wheat crops, often murdering Iroquois women and children at the same time, and food was soon in short supply. Molly, however, gave hope to her hungry, despairing people. Over and over again the Iroquois were told they would return to their own lands at the end of the war.

She also would not allow angry, young warriors to attack enemy settlements without their war leader, Joseph Brant. She convinced them that they could not win the war with unplanned, unprepared raids. Molly also encouraged the other Clan Mothers to keep their people strong allies of Britain.

The commander of Fort Haldimand claimed that Molly Brant's ability to control her people was "far superior to that of all their chiefs put together."

## BETRAYAL

The American Patriot forces won the war in 1781, but it took two more years for British and Americans to write the peace treaty that would set the boundaries of the new United States of America.

The Iroquois were outraged when they finally heard the treaty terms—all their lands had been handed over to their enemies, the Americans.

"How could the British King give away land that did not belong to him?" the angry Iroquois people demanded. There was only one answer. The British had completely ignored the rights and demands of the Iroquois, their courageous, long-time allies.

The commanders of the British forts in North America, were also shocked by the peace treaty terms. They were terrified that the Iroquois would attack British forts in revenge.

Molly was enraged by the betrayal. Her beautiful Mohawk Valley was lost forever and her people were now powerless refugees. After much thought, however, Molly decided that no good would come of the war-weary Iroquois fighting yet another war. She counseled her people not to attack the British.

## UPPER CANADA

The British offered their Iroquois allies lands in the new province of Upper Canada to replace some of the lands they lost in the American Revolution. Some Iroquois settled along the Grand River and some settled in the Bay of Quinte area.

**A painting of Cataraqui (now Kingston, Ontario) where Molly Brant settled after the American Revolution.**

The British government gave Molly, as the widow of Sir William Johnson, land grants in Upper Canada to make up for the large land holdings she had lost in the Mohawk Valley. Molly decided to settle at Cataraqui (now Kingston, Ontario) so that she could be sure the Iroquois settlers in the Bay of Quinte area were properly treated by the superintendent of Indian Affairs. As a reward for her many services during the war, the British government paid for the boarding school education of Molly's children, gave her a yearly pension and a comfortable house at Cataraqui.

## SICK AT HEART

Molly watched with despair as south of the new border the Americans pushed farther and farther west into the Ohio River country of the Shawnees, Miamis and the Delawares. She was sickened by the news of the defeat and slaughter of the Miamis by the American general "Mad" Anthony Wayne in 1794.

The American government worried about the possibility of attack from the Iroquois who now lived outside the American border and therefore outside American control. Believing other Iroquois would return if the Brants did, the American government tried to lure Molly back by offering her a large sum of money if she returned to live in the United States and under American control. Molly refused the offer with contempt.

Molly became ill in 1795 as she worried over the bleak future of North America's First Nations. Later, her cousin accused her of putting her own interests first and of being a traitor to her people. Molly angrily denied the claim but his words caused her deep sorrow.

Sick at heart over the fate of her people, Molly died a year later at the age of sixty. Molly Brant was a strong, intelligent woman with great power and influence during a difficult time in Iroquois history.

Further Suggested Reading:

Johnson, Jean. *Wilderness Women*. Toronto: Peter Martin Associates Ltd., 1976.

Robinson, Helen Caistor. *Mistress Molly*. Toronto: Dundurn Press, 1980.

# CHAPTER 6

## HERO OF THE WAR OF 1812

# LAURA INGERSOLL SECORD

## —————— (1775 - 1868) ——————

**Mrs Secord arrived at my Station about sunset of an excessively warm day, after having walked about twelve miles which I at the time thought was an exertion which a person of her slender frame and delicate appearance was unequal to make.**

—Lieutenant James FitzGibbon

*Laura's dress was ripped and spattered with mud and her bare feet were bleeding. Exhausted and in pain, she looked around the gloomy forest in despair. It was almost dark. How could she find FitzGibbon and warn him of the danger?*

*Laura limped out into a clearing and froze. There, in the moonlight, was a native encampment! The warriors gave a menacing shout and quickly surrounded her.*

*Laura struggled to keep her terror from showing. The Mohawks were allies of the British and Canadians. If these men were Mohawks, they would help her. But what if they were not Mohawks?*

*She had to take a chance. Laura Secord took a deep breath and lifted her chin proudly. "FitzGibbon," she said firmly. "I must see Lieutenant FitzGibbon!"*

## AMERICAN BORN

Laura Ingersoll was born in 1775 in the state of Massachusetts, in the United States. Laura's father, Thomas Ingersoll, was a major in the American army. As a Patriot he fought against the British during the American Revolution.

After the American Revolution, however, there were bands of men roaming the Massachusetts countryside demanding lodging and money at gunpoint. The Ingersolls were alarmed by the growing lawlessness and violence they saw around them. They decided to leave the United States and move north to the British province of Upper Canada (now Ontario).

**Queenston, Upper Canada (now Ontario), was an important place in 1812. It lay at one end of a busy portage route that curved around the huge Niagara Falls.**

Good, cheap land was for sale in Upper Canada.

At the age of eighteen, Laura moved with her family to the bustling port of Queenston, located on the Niagara River below the thundering Niagara Falls. Laura's father later settled in another area of Upper Canada. Ingersoll, Ontario, is named after Thomas Ingersoll.

While in Queenston, Laura met and married a young merchant by the name of James Secord. James Secord's father was a Loyalist who had fought on the British side in the American Revolution. James, as a young child, had been among the first of thousands of Loyalist refugees from the American Revolution to arrive in Upper Canada.

Laura and James had five children and owned a prosperous store in Queenston. War with the United States, however, quickly turned Laura's world upside down.

## WAR WITH THE UNITED STATES

The War of 1812 grew out of a conflict in the early 1800s known as the

Napoleonic Wars. These wars were between France, led by the Emperor Napoleon, and Great Britain. The United States was not at war with France and wanted to continue to sell its goods to both France and Great Britain. Great Britain, fighting for her life against an enemy that had already conquered much of Europe, used the powerful British navy to prevent American goods and supplies from reaching France and her allies. Some British ships also stopped and boarded American ships looking for runaways from the British navy. All these actions angered the United States.

As well, some Americans thought those who lived in the Canadas would welcome invading American soldiers and cheerfully join the United States without a fight. In 1812 Americans declared war on Great Britain and attacked Upper Canada and Lower Canada because they were British colonies.

Britain was not able to spare many career soldiers to defend the Canadas. However Canada's European settlers, many of them Loyalists

**A painting of Niagara (now Niagara-on-the-Lake, Ontario) around 1790. Fort Niagara can be seen in the distance on the other side of the river. Laura's Loyalist husband, James Secord, was three when he arrived at Fort Niagara in 1776.**

**A painting of the Battle of Queenston Heights. Americans realized if they controlled Queenston, they could stop the movement of goods and soldiers between the upper Great Lakes and the rest of Upper and Lower Canada (now Ontario and Quebec).**

and children of Loyalists, such as James Secord, were not alone in their fight. Britain's traditional allies, the Iroquois or Six Nations agreed to fight the Americans. As well, black Canadians formed their own unit, called the Company of Colored Men, to defend their country against the American invasion.

## THE BATTLE OF QUEENSTON HEIGHTS

When the United States declared war in 1812, James Secord joined his regiment, the 1st Lincoln Militia. Just before dawn on 13 October 1812, American troops rowed across the Niagara River and attacked Queenston. Laura awoke to the sound of cannons firing and quickly moved her five children, ranging in ages from thirteen to two, to a farmhouse. There she and the children waited for news about James who was fighting in the battle nearby.

The sight of Six Nations Mohawk warriors, allies of the British and skilled fighters, had terrified many of the American volunteer soldiers. The Mohawk war cries, echoing across the Niagara River caused some American soldiers to stay put on the American side of the river. Unfortunately, General Brock, the popular British general in charge of the

British and Canadian forces, was killed in battle that day by an American sharpshooter. News of Brock's death made the British and Canadian forces lose heart and for a while it seemed the Americans would win.

Then came the news that James Secord was lying on the battlefield. He was wounded and calling for Laura's help.

## THE RESCUE OF JAMES

Laura picked her way through the battlefield, past bleeding, twisted bodies, searching for her husband. When she found James, he had been shot in the shoulder and in the knee and was unable to walk. Suddenly three American soldiers appeared, and pushing Laura aside, prepared to beat James to death. Laura screamed in horror and, throwing herself across James, kicked out at the men.

An American officer, hearing Laura's scream, appeared. He was shocked that his soldiers would try to kill an injured man and had James carried back to the Secord house in Queenston.

In the end, the Battle of Queenston Heights, as it was later called, was won by the British-Canadian forces. Brock's second in command, General Sheaffe, rallied his soldiers and drove the American invaders back across the Niagara River.

The battle, however, financially ruined the Secords. Their home and store in Queenston had been looted during the battle and most of their

**The house where Laura Secord began her famous walk. It has been preserved as the Laura Secord Homestead in Queenston, Ontario.**

things stolen or destroyed. As well, James' war wounds were serious and never completely healed.

## UNWANTED GUESTS

The following May, Queenston was again invaded by the United States and this time the Americans won. In the area the Americans now controlled, all Canadian men over eighteen were marched away as prisoners of war. However, because James Secord's war wounds meant he was still not able to walk, the Americans decided he was not dangerous. James was allowed to remain in his Queenston home with Laura and their children.

American troops took control of the area and needed places to live. As a result, three American officers moved into the Secord house. The large Secord family was forced to live in only the kitchen and one bedroom of their own home.

The Secords also had to provide dinner for the three officers every day, and the American officers often discussed military matters as they sat around the table after their meal. Toward the end of June, the three officers invited the new American commander, Colonel Boerstler, to dine with them. The dinner was a great success and, as usual, the conversation soon turned to the war.

Laura overheard the Americans planning a surprise attack the next night on the Canadian forces near a place called Beaver Dams. The forces at Beaver Dams, under the command of Lieutenant FitzGibbon, were all that prevented the Americans from pushing right through the Niagara Peninsula and on to York (now Toronto, Ontario). It is possible that Laura memorized the details of the American battle plan, including the number of American troops and the types of weapons they would bring to the battle. The officers boasted the American troops would outnumber the Canadians ten to one in the upcoming attack.

James and Laura discussed the matter secretly. If Lieutenant FitzGibbon was warned, his men might be able to defeat the American forces. The Secords agreed that FitzGibbon must be told, but how? It would be a long and dangerous journey to the Decew House where FitzGibbon was stationed, and James was still unable to walk.

Laura, loyal to her adopted country, was determined to do her part. She decided she must be the one to warn FitzGibbon that the Americans were coming.

**The Decew house near Beaver Dams where Laura delivered her message to Lieutenant FitzGibbon.**

## 22 JUNE 1813

Laura began her thirty-two-kilometre walk the next day at four in the morning. She told the American sentry outside their home that she was walking to the village of St David's to visit her sick brother. Laura had dressed herself to look as if she was going for a social visit—her second best dress, low-buckled shoes, and a cotton sunbonnet. Her basket contained only tea, jam and bread, so the sentry believed her story and let her pass.

Once she arrived in St David's, she quickly visited her sick brother and then continued the trip accompanied by her twenty-year-old niece, Elizabeth Secord. The two women left the main road and traveled along a tiny path called the Old Swamp Road. It wandered across a frightening area known as the Black Swamp. Travel along the main road would have meant a shorter walk and easier walking conditions for them. Laura, however, knew American soldiers patrolling the road would be suspicious of anyone walking in the direction of the Canadian outpost at Beaver Dams. They would certainly be stopped and questioned. The two women could then be arrested and even shot as a spies. It was safer, Laura felt, to stay off the traveled roads. They would still, however, need to keep a sharp eye out for the rattlesnakes, wolves, wildcats and bears that lived in the area.

The June heat pressed in on Laura and Elizabeth as they picked their way through the Black Swamp. At one point the ground beneath their feet grew soft and they began to sink into the bog. Desperately they pulled themselves out by clinging to overhanging branches. One of Laura's shoes, however, was sucked down into the swamp.

The sun was high in the sky when Laura and Elizabeth stumbled out of the swamp. Time was running out for Laura, as she still had to climb the "Mountain" to find FitzGibbon. The Mountain was the local name for the Niagara Escarpment, which was a long, high ridge of land whose steep slopes were covered in forest.

## THE AMERICANS ARE COMING!

Laura's niece Elizabeth was too exhausted to continue, so she stayed behind at a nearby farm, while Laura, alone once more, set off to climb the Mountain. She had to cross the winding, rain-swollen Ten Mile Creek twice along the way. The first time, she waded across the creek and lost her other shoe. The second time she crossed by inching across a fallen tree trunk. Her feet were gashed and bleeding, and she wrapped them in strips of cloth torn from her petticoats.

When Laura finally climbed to the top of the Mountain, she had no idea how to locate FitzGibbon. She stumbled through a beech woods and then out into a clearing. Suddenly she was surrounded by Mohawks and Caughnawagas—loyal Six Nations allies of the British and an important part of FitzGibbon's forces. Exhausted after her eighteen-hour-walk, and terrified by the warriors' weapons and fierce appearance, Laura nonetheless persuaded them to take her to FitzGibbon at the Decew House.

FitzGibbon, who later described the thirty-eight-year-old woman as being slender and delicate looking, was amazed at the distance Laura had traveled. Laura probably gave him a detailed account of the American troops and weapons that Colonel Boerstler planned to use in the surprise attack. FitzGibbon thanked Laura and made immediate plans for the upcoming battle.

When the Americans arrived, FitzGibbon's fifty soldiers and two hundred warriors were ready for the attack. The American troops were lured into an ambush. The Mohawks and Caughnawagas shot down American soldiers with such deadly accuracy that FitzGibbon's own regiment did not fire a single shot during the entire battle! It was a tremendous victory for FitzGibbon because the American Colonel Boerstler and all but six of his soldiers were captured by a much smaller force. The American attempt to control the Niagara Peninsula ended with a crushing American defeat in the Battle of Beaver Dams.

After the battle, Laura quietly left the Decew House and returned to Queenston.

Lieutenant FitzGibbon, for his part, was given credit for his brilliant battle plan. Laura Secord, however, was ignored. She received no recognition for her heroic, eighteen-hour-walk until she was eighty-five.

## THE WAR YEARS

During the war, it was in the best interests of the Secord family that no mention be made of Laura's part in the Battle of Beaver Dams. The Secords lived so close to the border that it would have been easy for Americans to take revenge on Laura and her family.

The Americans were enraged by their embarrassing defeat at Beaver Dams. In December of that year, American troops burned nearby Niagara-on-the-Lake to the ground, and still later, the nearby village of St David's. The Secords, like other families in the area, opened their small Queenston home up to those who were now homeless. Laura with five children, a sick husband and numerous houseguests under her roof, managed as best she could until the war, and its terrible destruction, ended.

## A STRUGGLE TO SURVIVE

After the war ended in 1814, the Secords struggled to pay the bills. James' war wounds continued to cause him pain and he had trouble earning a living. As well, two more Secord children were born after the war.

Using his war record and a letter from James FitzGibbon, now a colonel, verifying Laura's brave walk and her part in the victory at Beaver Dams, James Secord finally obtained the position of customs collector. Once Laura helped James capture a dangerous gang of smugglers by carrying a gun and dressing up as a man.

Over the years the Secords, as was the custom of the day, requested money or some sort of government post as a reward for Laura's services to her country. The requests, supported by letters from James FitzGibbon, were always denied.

When James Secord died in 1841, Laura was left penniless at the age of sixty-five. She struggled to support herself by selling her own needlework and by running a school.

## RECOGNITION AT LAST

When she was seventy-eight, a newspaper article told Laura's story and her fame began to spread. Eventually Prince Edward (later King Edward VII) heard her story and sent Laura one hundred pounds as a reward for her bravery. She was eighty-five at the time. It had taken the government almost fifty years to recognize her heroic contribution.

Laura Ingersoll Secord, one of Canada's best known heroes, died in 1868 at the age of ninety-three.

Further Suggested Reading:

Bassett, John M. and A. Roy Petrie. *Laura Secord*. Toronto: Fitzhenry & Whiteside, 1974.

Robinson, Helen Caistor. *Laura*. Toronto: Dundurn Press, 1981.

# CHAPTER 7

## THE LAST OF THE BEOTHUK

# SHAWNADITHIT

## ———— (1800 - 1829) ————

**She was very gentle and . . . was adept at drawing or copying anything.**
**—Mrs Gill**

*The three women, shivering in the bitter cold of winter, gazed at each other in despair. They were dying of starvation and everyone else in the village was dead or missing.*

*Fifteen villagers—dead this winter, Shawnadithit thought wearily. Men, women and children—she had helped to bury them all. Now her own mother and sister had some strange illness— they coughed and sometimes spit up blood. Without proper food, Shawnadithit knew the others would soon die. Then she would be alone.*

*Perhaps the three of them could make it down to the coast, she thought. They were too weak to catch a deer or a seal, but they might be able to fish. Traveling to the coast was risky, for any "buggishaman"—the Beothuk name for the dreaded white invaders of their land—would kill them on sight.*

*There was, however, no other choice. The three women began the long journey toward the Atlantic Ocean.*

## THE WORLD OF THE BEOTHUKS

Before the arrival of the Europeans, Newfoundland's forests and oceans teemed with life. For almost two thousand years one of the First Nations had lived in this rich land, eating and preserving the many foods that each season offered. The people called themselves Beothuk which means "people" in their language. The Beothuk hunted and gathered as a group and shared the food equally. In the spring and summer they set up villages along the coast and ate fresh seal meat, Atlantic salmon, lobsters, clams, and mussels. Some of the summer food was preserved and put away for the winter when finding food was difficult.

In their birch-bark canoes the Beothuk paddled out to sea islands where they gathered seabird eggs. Often they boiled the eggs in birch bark containers then dried and powdered the yolks. The result was a nourishing food that was easy to store and to carry.

In the fall the Beothuk moved inland and built winter villages. They hunted ducks, geese, caribou and small mammals such as beaver. They carefully saved the meat for the long, cold winter months and made the skins and furs into warm clothing. The Beothuk then spent much of the long winter inside their houses where they held council meetings or celebrated with feasts, games and stories.

The Beothuk's ability to gather food, however, changed with the arrival of British settlers in the 1700s.

## SLAVES

The Beothuk covered their clothes, bodies and weapons with a mixture of red ochre and oil. This mixture protected their skin against insects in the summer and cold in the winter. The Beothuk also believed the red dye protected the life of the wearer. Early Europeans saw the "red skins" of the Beothuk and called them Red Indians.

Canada's First Nations were often as different from each other in both appearance and custom as the French were from the Finns. The Beothuk, as a group were tall, white-skinned people with black hair and eyes.

The first experiences of the Beothuk with Europeans were bitter ones. The slave trade was profitable at the time and white-skinned slaves brought even higher prices than African slaves. The Europeans thought the Beothuk would be valuable in the slave trade once the red ochre dye was washed off their white skins. In 1500, Portuguese merchants lured friendly Beothuk onto their ships then carried off whole Beothuk families to sell in the slave markets of Europe.

From that point on, the Beothuk distrusted all Europeans and, realizing their own weapons were no match for European guns, did their best to avoid the hated *buggishaman*.

## HATRED AND SUSPICION

In the 1700s, however, thousands of British settled along the Newfoundland coast, often in the same bays and inlets where the Beothuk had, for hundreds of years, set up their summer villages. The Beothuk were soon cut off from the best fishing and hunting spots on the seashore by the unfriendly British settlements.

Forced to stay inland where there was less food, the Beothuk began to starve. They also began to die from new diseases that the British had carried to the island—horrible diseases such as smallpox and a deadly lung disease called tuberculosis.

The Beothuk saw the British settlers as invaders and thieves of Beothuk land. They prized, however, the iron tools of the British and sometimes quietly raided white settlements by night. While their enemy slept, the Beothuk seized useful items such as iron, rope, and cloth then slipped back to their inland villages.

The British who traveled inland in the winter months trapping animals for the fur trade with Europe, wanted to take over all Beothuk hunting grounds. As well, the British settlers, angered by the night raids of the Red Indians, viewed the Beothuk as dangerous thieves and would not hesitate to kill any Beothuk on sight. Sometimes the British settlers attacked Beothuk villages, stealing Beothuk furs and killing the inhabitants. The Beothuk, given the chance, would also kill unwary British men. For years, each group viewed the other with hatred and suspicion.

## A REWARD FOR THEIR CAPTURE

When Shawnadithit was born around the year 1800, the Beothuk were a dying race. There were less than two hundred people left in her village beside Red Indian Lake.

While Shawnadithit was still a girl, however, the government of Newfoundland, suddenly alarmed that the Beothuk would soon all be dead, offered a large cash reward to anyone who captured and brought in a live Beothuk. Their plan was to treat the Beothuk captive in a kindly way, teach the Beothuk to speak English and then return the captive, along with many gifts, to a Beothuk village. The government hoped that the Beothuk would then see that the *buggishaman* now wanted to be friends and help the Beothuk.

The plan was a disaster. The Beothuk suddenly found themselves hunted down by fur trappers and fishermen who did not care how many Beothuk people they killed in a fight as long as one could be kidnapped and carried away for the reward money.

## CHILD OF SORROW

As a child, Shawnadithit had been shot by a trapper and wounded in the hand and leg as she washed food in a stream. By crawling away she managed to escape, but she carried the scars all her life.

She also saw her aunt, Demasduwit, captured and carried off by British men eager for reward money. The whole village had run away at the sight of the hated *buggishaman* , but Demasduwit, who was carrying her baby, could not run as quickly and was caught. When Demasduwit's husband came to her aid in a peaceful manner, he was stabbed in the

A picture of Demasduwit, the aunt of Shawnadithit. Early Europeans thought the Beothuk were an attractive race of people.

back, then shot and killed by the invaders. Demasduwit was dragged away into captivity. Her baby son, who had been left behind, died a few days later.

Demasduwit, who was renamed Mary March by the British settlers, was taught English and taken to St John's where she was sketched by Lady Hamilton at the governor's home. Within a year of her capture, however, she died of tuberculosis.

Meanwhile the Beothuk at Red Indian Lake continued to die of starvation and disease at an alarming rate. Shawnadithit grew into a young woman, but she knew she would never marry and have children— there were no eligible men left alive.

## DOOMED VILLAGE

By March of 1823 the few Beothuk still alive were desperate for food. Shawnadithit's uncle and cousin decided to travel to the sea coast where they hoped to find food. They knew they might be shot by a *buggishaman* along the way, but decided to take that chance.

Shawnadithit's mother and sister were now ill with tuberculosis so their family remained at the village. One day, however, Shawnadithit's father went out alone to hunt and did not return. The three women decided he had died.

Hunger forced the women to follow the others to the sea coast in search of food. Along the way they stumbled across the bodies of Shawnadithit's uncle and female cousin lying in the snow shot and killed by the *buggishaman*. Women were important in Beothuk society, and it was unthinkable to kill any woman. What kind of people would kill like this, the women must have asked themselves.

## CAPTIVES

Grief-stricken, the three starving women decided they could take no more. They would give themselves up to a *buggishaman* who would shoot them on the spot and put them out of their misery. When, however, they gave themselves up to a red-bearded trapper—one they had seen murder other Beothuk—he did not shoot them. Instead, the trapper forced the surprised women to march along with him; he wanted to collect the reward money.

The group had not traveled far beside a frozen river when they heard a shout behind them. Shawnadithit saw her father being chased toward them by another British trapper. Her father was still alive!

First Mothers: An Assiniboine mother with her child in a baby swing.

▼

▲

First Mothers: A Flathead mother and her baby. Instead of using diapers, native mothers stuffed baby carriers with soft, dry moss. The moss was thrown away when it became dirty.

**First Mothers: Lummi**

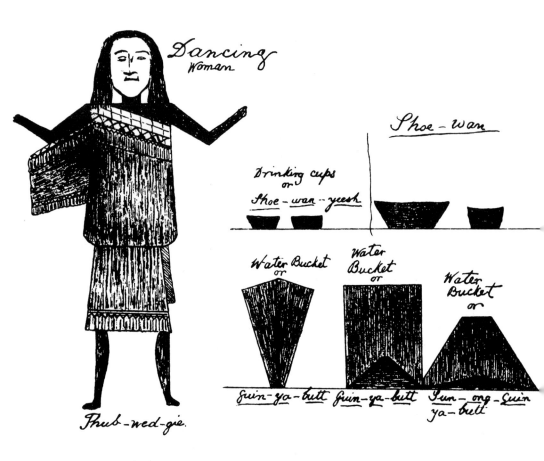

**Shawnadithit's pictures of the Beothuk way of life helped William Cormack learn about Beothuk traditions and culture.**

## MORE TRAGEDY

In a flash Shawnadithit's joy changed to anguish. The red-bearded trapper raised his musket. Shawnadithit's father saw the gun, and, trapped between two armed *buggishaman*, turned and ran across the ice-covered river. The ice broke and Shawnadithit watched with horror as her father sank beneath the swirling water and drowned.

The three starving women, numb with despair, were fed and cared for by the British settlers. Shawnadithit's mother and sister, however, soon died of tuberculosis.

Shawnadithit was now alone.

## ALONE WITH THE BUGGISHAMAN

For five years Shawnadithit worked as an unpaid servant for a British settler family who called her Nancy April. She loved the family's children and was a good worker. Sometimes, however, Shawnadithit suffered from periods of sadness and despair. When this happened she would wander out into the woods where she believed she talked and laughed with the spirits of her mother and sister. The belief that she was visited by her dead mother and sister helped the lonely woman to live with her sorrow.

## CONCERN FOR THE BEOTHUK

A growing number of Newfoundlanders became distressed by the plight of the Beothuk people. A Newfoundlander by the name of William Cormack traveled inland across Newfoundland hoping to contact and help the Beothuk. He had, however, been unable to find any Beothuk still alive. When Cormack finally heard about Shawnadithit, he had her brought to St John's in 1828. He believed she was the last of her race and wanted Shawnadithit to teach him about the Beothuk.

## LAST DAYS

Shawnadithit was a talented artist and drew pictures and maps for Cormack. She taught him Beothuk words and talked about her people, their beliefs and their way of life. Cormack wrote down what Shawnadithit told him and made careful notes on her maps and sketches. Although some of Cormack's notes have been lost, much of what we know today about the Beothuk is based upon Shawnadithit's talks with the sympathetic William Cormack. She always wept when she spoke about the last days of her people.

Sadly, when Shawnadithit arrived in St John's, she was already infected with the lung disease that had killed her mother, sister and aunt. Ten months later, Shawnadithit, the last of the Beothuk, died of tuberculosis. She was twenty-nine.

Further Suggested Reading:

Marshall, Ingeborg. *The Beothuk of Newfoundland*. St John's, Newfoundland: Breakwater Books, 1989.

# CHAPTER 8

## THEY CALLED HER MOSES

# HARRIET TUBMAN DAVIS

## (1820 - 1913)

There's *two* things I've got a *right* to, and these are Death or Liberty—one or the other I mean to have.

—Harriet Tubman Davis

*Harriet woke in her seat with a start. The two white men across the aisle were talking about her.*

*"Wonder if that's the woman they're lookin' for?" said the one. He pointed to a wanted poster in his hand.*

*"Let's grab her," whispered the other. "Look at the size of the reward. Says here they'll pay $12,000 for the capture of Harriet Tubman."*

*Harriet coolly reached into her shabby bag and pulled out a book. She opened it and sat very still, pretending to read. Across the aisle, the men looked disappointed. "That can't be the woman," one of them muttered. "The one we want can't read or write."*

*Harriet Tubman rode the rest of the train trip in peace. "Guess I'm holding this book the right way up," she chuckled to herself.*

### THE TROUBLE I SEE

Nobody knows the trouble I see,
Nobody knows but Jesus.
—Spiritual

In 1820, Harriet Tubman was born a slave in the slave state of Maryland. She grew up hating slavery with a passion. At the age of seven, Harriet was sent to work in the plantation fields as a field hand. Like the other field hands, Harriet spent sunup to sundown plowing the land, splitting firewood and cutting hay. As the slaves worked, they sang their work songs, known as sorrow songs or spirituals, under the watchful eye of a boss or overseer. The overseer was there to make sure the slaves worked hard and did not try to escape from their life of endless, unpaid labour.

Overseers believed that quiet slaves were thinking about how to escape so the overseers often forced the slaves to sing as they worked. White overseers and white owners, however, did not realize that there were messages hidden inside the spirituals that the slaves created and sang.

## AN UNFRIENDLY WORLD

I'm a-rolling, I'm a-rolling,
I'm a-rolling through an unfriendly world.
—Spiritual

HARRIET TUBMAN.

Like most slaves, Harriet was not taught to read or write. It was, in many slave states, against the law to teach a slave to read or write. The punishment for teaching a slave was life imprisonment or even death!

The reasons for these laws were simple—educated slaves were more difficult to control and more likely to escape. Educated slaves could read road signs and had a better chance of

**Although she was told a woman could not become a conductor on the Underground Railroad, Harriet Tubman Davis became the most successful conductor of them all.**

making their way to freedom without being caught.

At the age of fifteen, Harriet helped another slave to escape. An angry white overseer smashed Harriet on the head with an iron weight, knocking her unconscious for many days. When Harriet finally recovered, she had a deep dent in her forehead where the skull bone had been crushed, and she also suffered from blinding headaches and unusual sleeping spells for the rest of her life. From then on, Harriet would suddenly black out and fall asleep, no matter where she was or what she was doing. The sudden blackouts could happen as often as three or four times a day. She could fall asleep in the middle of a sentence or even while standing up. Then, just as suddenly, Harriet would wake up and continue as if nothing had happened.

## STEAL AWAY HOME

Steal away, steal away home.
I ain't got long to stay here.
                    —Spiritual

Some slaves were lucky enough to be set free by their owners, but this
rarely happened. Most slaves, as well as their children and grandchildren,
remained slaves from birth until death.

Escape from slavery was difficult. Because of their skin colour,
black slaves stood out from the largely white population. It was difficult
for a slave to slip away and start a new life in another slave state without
being noticed by the white community. A runaway slave's only hope,
therefore, was to escape to an area where slavery was against the law.

In 1793 the United States passed its first Fugitive Slave Act which
made it a crime for anyone to help a runaway slave. However, the
American states which did not have slavery ("free states") generally paid
no attention to this act. Slaves who were able to escape to free states such
as Pennsylvania and New York could live there as if they were free men
and women.

As well, in 1793 Upper Canada (later called Canada West and today
Ontario) passed a law which brought a gradual stop to slavery in the
province and slavery was completely ended in the British Empire 1834.
As a result, once fugitive slaves arrived in Upper Canada they were free.

Although Harriet was unable to read or write, she had heard about
the places where a slave could be free, and she had often thought about
escape. When Harriet found out her owner was planning to sell her,
Harriet escaped to Pennsylvania.

## THE GOSPEL TRAIN'S A-COMIN'

The Gospel train's a-comin'
I hear it just at hand,
I hear the car wheels rollin'
And rumbling through the land.
                    —Spiritual

Harriet escaped into Pennsylvania by way of the Underground Railroad.
The Underground Railroad was not under the ground and was not really
a railroad. Although the spirituals sometimes called it a train or a chariot,
the Underground Railroad was a group of people, black and white, who
secretly helped escaped slaves on their dangerous journey to freedom.

The people who were a part of the Underground Railroad, however,

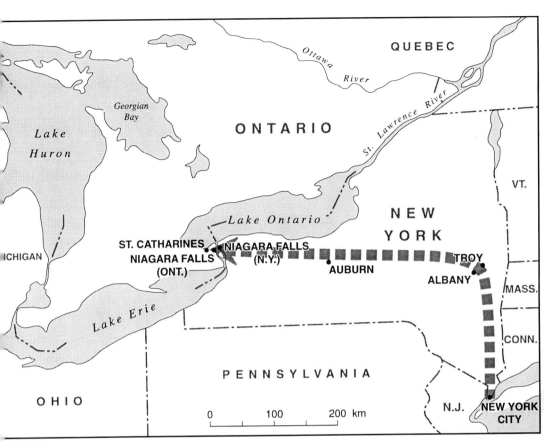

One of the Underground Railroad routes that
Harriet used to bring her "passengers" to Canada.

used railroad words as code names. Escaped slaves were called passengers, the houses where slaves were hidden on their journey were called stations, people who hid the slaves were stationmasters and stationmistresses,and the guides who led the slaves from one safe house to the next were called conductors.

## WHO'S GOING WITH ME?

When that old chariot comes
I'm going to leave you.
I'm bound for the promised land.
Friends, I'm going to leave you.
When that old chariot comes,
Who's going with me?
          —Spiritual

**The first American Fugitive Slave Act in 1793 caused many runaway slaves to feel unsafe anywhere in the United States. Some escaped to Upper Canada to live in freedom. This woman was painted in Niagara Falls in 1838.**

When Harriet arrived in Philadelphia she enjoyed her freedom, but she was lonely and missed her family. In Philadelphia she learned more about the Underground Railroad and how conductors often went back into the South to steal their own families away from slavery. Harriet's heart leapt at the thought of bringing her family to live with her in a free state.

The members of the Underground Railroad told her that women could not be conductors, but Harriet knew better.

"Nobody asked whether I was man or woman when they put an ax in my hand or tied me by the waist to a mule," Harriet declared. "I've been doing man's work all my life. I'm not afraid." She worked at a number of jobs—laundress, cook, seamstress–and saved enough to buy something for her new career—a gun!

Harriet soon became the most successful conductor of them all.

## NO HIDING PLACE

No hiding place down here,
Down here,
No hiding place down here.
I went to the rock to hide my face
The rock it said "no hiding place,
No hiding place down here."
—Spiritual

Harriet began rescuing members of her family, one after another, as well as any other slaves who dared to come with her on the dangerous journey north to freedom. After she made three such trips into the slave states, in

**Black Loyalists arrived in Canada during the American Revolution. The people in the above painting, set near Halifax, Nova Scotia, are probably descendents of black Loyalists.**

1850 the United States passed a second Fugitive Slave Act. This new law ordered marshals and deputies in the free states to hunt down runaway slaves in their area and return them to their owners in the slave states. Those officials who refused could be fined one thousand dollars. Now there was no hiding place left in the United States for Harriet, or any other escaped slave.

Canada became the only place where escaped slaves could live in freedom because escaped slaves could not be removed from Canada against their will. So after 1850, all routes of the Underground Railroad traveled north into Canada.

## STRAIGHT TO CANADA

Farewell old master,
This is enough for me,
I'm going straight to Canada
Where coloured men are free.
                    —Spiritual

A few spirituals, such as the one above, were never sung in front of overseers and slave owners. Most spirituals did not dare to openly mention Canada. Instead, the slaves sang about escaping to Canada by using code names such as Heaven, or the Promised Land or Canaan Land.

Harriet began leading her passengers north to Canada and altogether brought more than three hundred escaped slaves to Canada, including her elderly parents and four of her brothers. She carried out each rescue with military precision and care, leaving nothing to chance. Most of her trips ended at the town of St Catharines, Canada West (now Ontario), which was the Canadian centre of her Underground Railroad activities.

Harriet moved to St Catharines and rented a boarding house which she used as a shelter for the new

**Some routes of the Underground Railroad ended in the Canadian mid-west. Above is a photograph of a pioneer woman in Pincher Creek, Alberta.**

refugees. She usually spent a few months in Canada after each journey to help her passengers become familiar with their new home. Harriet also used her time in Canada to plan further rescue missions.

Her house was located behind the British Methodist Episcopal Church, which was an important religious and social centre for St Catharines' growing black population. The BME Church, which Harriet attended, is still standing today.

# BLACK MOSES

Go down Moses,
Way down in Egypt's land.
Tell old Pharaoh,
Let my people go.
          —Spiritual

Harriet made eleven or so trips from Canada into the United States to bring slaves back to Canada and freedom. The roads in the United States were regularly patrolled by slave catchers who wanted to claim the reward money offered for the capture of escaped slaves. To trick the slave catchers, Harriet often used simple disguises and forged documents on her journeys. She also sang spirituals as signals and passwords.

Each trip meant danger and hardship for Harriet and her passengers. Often they hid in damp cellars underneath cabins, in secret rooms in houses and barns, inside hollowed out haystacks in the fields, and up inside chimneys. As well, they often travelled by night through dense woods and waded across icy-cold, waist-deep rivers to throw the slave catchers' blood hounds off their scent. Harriet would find her way by watching the night sky for the Northern star or by feeling the trunks of the trees for moss to discover which way was north.

Harriet helped to carry small children and babies and went without food when there was not enough to go around. She was a strong leader— allowing no fires, no matter how cold and wet they became.

Harriet did not allow any of her passengers to turn back. Harriet knew slaves who returned to their plantations could be beaten or tortured until they told all they knew about the Underground Railroad and its members. When anyone tried to turn back, Harriet simply pulled out her gun and said, "Dead men tell no tales. Go on or die!" Her word was law and not one of her passengers was ever caught.

Harriet's fame spread through the slave states. The slaves knew the Bible story of a man named Moses who led his people out of slavery to freedom in Canaan, which was the Promised Land. Soon Harriet became known as Moses or Black Moses. Slaves longing to escape felt a thrill of joy when they heard the whispered words "Get ready to leave. Moses is coming tonight." They knew Harriet would lead any slave who dared, to Canada and freedom.

The slave owners also began to hear about Harriet Tubman—this mysterious woman who stole their slaves away from them right under their noses. They offered rewards for her capture—dead or alive—as high as twelve thousand dollars. The wanted posters read:

## HARRIET TUBMAN

## WANTED DEAD OR ALIVE

## A PLAIN WOMAN, SHORT OF STATURE, UPPER FRONT TEETH MISSING, WITH A HABIT OF ABRUPTLY FALLING ASLEEP. LOOKS HARMLESS, BUT SHE CARRIES A PISTOL

Harriet Tubman, a slave who could not read or write and who suffered from unpredictable sleeping spells, was never caught. If Harriet had been caught, her friends believed she would have been burned alive as an example to other runaway slaves.

## FREE AT LAST

Free at last!
Free at last!
Thank God Almighty,
We are free at last!
   —Spiritual

With the outbreak of the American Civil War in 1861 Harriet returned to the United States and joined the Union Army. She worked for three years as a Union nurse, scout and spy and became the only woman in American military history to plan and conduct an armed expedition against enemy forces. Her successful expedition would later be known as the Combahee River Raid.

At the end of the Civil War slavery was abolished in 1865 by the Thirteenth Amendment to the American Constitution. American slaves were free at last and there was no longer a need for the Underground Railroad.

## CARRY ME HOME

Swing low, sweet chariot,
Comin' for to carry me home.
   —Spiritual

After the Civil War, Harriet lived in the town of Auburn, New York. In Auburn, Harriet was close to many of her friends from the Underground Railroad. She struggled to made a living by traveling door-to-door selling the vegetables she had grown herself. Today her home in Auburn is a museum.

In 1869 Harriet married Nelson Davis who had fought in the Civil War in the 8th US Colored Infantry Volunteers. Nelson's health was poor and he died of tuberculosis, a lung disease, in 1890.

A woman named Sarah Bradford wrote a book about Harriet's incredible life which was published in 1869. Queen Victoria, the Queen of Great Britain and Canada, read the book and was impressed. In 1897 the Queen sent Harriet a letter and gifts of a black silk shawl and a silver Diamond Jubilee medal.

One of her friends and admirers, William Henry Seward, a governor of New York state, a United States senator and a secretary of state, once wrote about Harriet, "I have known her long and a nobler, higher spirit, or a truer, seldom dwells in the human form."

To the very end Harriet remained active by fund-raising for schools for black children. She also believed women should have the right to vote. A month before she died, Harriet said to a friend, "Tell the women to stand together."

As friends sang Harriet's favourite spiritual *Swing Low, Sweet Chariot*, the woman they called Moses died on 10 March 1913. She was ninety-three.

Further Suggested Reading:

Sterling, Dorothy. *Freedom Train*. New York: Scholastic Inc.

Taylor, M. W. *Harriet Tubman*. New York: Chelsea House Publishers, 1991.

Mary Shadd was the first black woman in North America
to establish and edit a weekly newspaper.

# CHAPTER 9

## EDITOR AND ACTIVIST

# MARY SHADD CARY

## —————— (1823 - 1893) ——————

**With voice and pen she is equally eloquent.**

**—Frederick Douglass**

*"Come with me I'll save you!" Mary whispered to the frightened child. The boy looked up at her and nodded. Mary grabbed his hand and together they raced along the dusty street. Behind them, the two slave catchers bellowed in surprise and then took up the chase.*

*Out of breath, Mary slowed down in front of a large building. "We'll get help in the courthouse," Mary gasped as they staggered up its steps. Once inside the building Mary violently rang its huge bell. As the bell rang out its alarm, the townspeople of Chatham quickly gathered at the court house.*

*Mary pointed at the two men who had chased her. "They are slave catchers," she shouted with contempt, "and they are trying to drag a child back to the United States to be a slave!"*

*The angry murmur from the crowd rose to a roar. Someone screamed "Grab them!" and the crowd rushed forward.*

*The slave catchers turned and ran for their lives.*

## FREE BLACKS IN A SLAVE STATE

Mary Ann Shadd was born in Wilmington, Delaware, on 9 October 1823, the eldest in a family of thirteen children. Although slavery was legal in the American state of Delaware, Mary's parents, Abraham Shadd and Harriet Parnell Shadd, were free blacks. Their children, therefore, were also free.

The Shadd family members were respectable and hard working. Secretly, however, the Shadds were in a dangerous business. Slaves could free themselves by escaping from their masters and travelling to a state where slavery was against the law. As they traveled through a slave state, however, runaway slaves needed safe houses where they could secretly eat and rest.

By the 1830s the secret organization that had sprung up to help runaway slaves was called the Underground Railroad for, like a train, it quickly moved people to their destinations. The safe houses along the routes were called stations and the people who ran them were called stationmasters.

Mary's parents were stationmasters for the Shadd home was a station on the Underground Railroad. As free blacks in a slave state, the Shadds took a terrible risk by hiding fugitive slaves in their home.

## MARY'S FIRST CAREER

Harriet and Abraham Shadd believed that blacks would achieve equality with their white neighbours through education, hard work and thrift. However, the slave state of Delaware did not allow black children to attend school. As a result, when Mary was ten, the Shadds moved to West Chester, in the free state of Pennsylvania. Mary completed her education in Pennsylvania then returned to Delaware where she opened a school for black children. She then taught in a number of schools in the northeastern United States.

## THE FUGITIVE SLAVE ACT

The northern states had long been a place where slaves who had escaped from their masters in the American slave states could feel free. However, the passage of the 1850 Fugitive Slave Act changed all that. This tough federal act meant that runaway slaves living in a free state remained the property of their slave owners. Federal authorities in the northern states were now duty-bound to return escaped slaves to their owners. As well, people caught helping fugitive slaves were fined so heavily that they were financially ruined.

Overnight the northern United States became unsafe, enemy territory for all escaped slaves. Blacks who had lived freely in the North for years could be kidnapped at any time and returned to slavery in the South.

Even free blacks, such as the Shadds, were not safe from legal kidnappings. Blacks accused of being runaway slaves were not given a jury trial or even allowed to speak in their own defense. There were cases of free blacks being forced into slavery by being kidnapped and returned to people who had never owned them.

Blacks now looked northward to Canada West (now Ontario) as a place where they could live in freedom. Slavery had been abolished in Canada for a number of years and, more importantly, escaped slaves could not be legally removed from Canadian soil.

## ON TO CANADA WEST

As a result of the Fugitive Slave Act, the Underground Railroad now ended in Canada West (now Ontario). Thousands of Americans—free blacks as well as fugitive slaves—began to pour into Canada West.

It had been against the law in many slave states to teach a slave to read or write. Once they reached Canada West, however, the black refugees, both young and old, were often eager to learn. The country needed more teachers and more schools to deal with the arrival of so many refugees.

Mary responded to the need by moving to Canada West in 1851 and setting up a school in Windsor—a busy hamlet of less than two hundred people. Windsor, located across the Detroit River from Detroit, Michigan, was the end of the Underground Railroad for many escaped slaves. The runaway slaves often arrived there with nothing but the ragged clothes on their backs. Mary soon discovered that Windsor's black community was poor and lived in overcrowded conditions.

Henry and Mary Bibb were the leaders of the local black community, and it was at their invitation that Mary had come to teach in Windsor. Once an escaped slave, Henry now published a newspaper called *The Voice of the Fugitive*.

Mary quickly set up a school in Windsor and just as quickly made enemies out of Henry and Mary Bibb.

## A DIFFERENCE OF OPINION

The abolitionists—people who believed that slavery was evil and must end—did not always agree on what was the best course of action for black Americans. Some believed blacks should move to Africa. Some, like Mary, believed blacks should move to Canada. Some, like the famous black writer and speaker Frederick Douglass, believed blacks should remain in the United States and fight to end slavery.

In Canada, the black community was also forced to make the type of decisions faced by all groups of newly arrived immigrants. Should they keep separate and apart from other Canadians? This would happen if they lived together in the same closed neighbourhoods, set up their own private churches and their own private schools. This approach, favoured by Henry and Mary Bibb, was called segregation.

Mary Shadd, however, claimed that segregation would cause blacks to be treated as second-rate citizens. She believed blacks in Canada should not cluster together but should spread out into the community and attend existing schools and churches. This approach was known as integration.

Therefore Mary's public refusal to teach at a "blacks only" school, began a struggle between Mary Shadd and Henry Bibb that would last until Henry's death in 1854.

## PRIVATE SCHOOLS

Although black children were entitled to attend public schools at no cost, often the black children were kept out of these schools on the feeble excuse that the black community should set up its own separate public schools.

Impoverished black communities were often unable to take the various legal steps necessary to get funding for their own public schools. It was therefore necessary for people like Mary Shadd to quickly set up private schools to give black children an education.

Mary's school was open to blacks and whites alike. However, white children could attend public school free of charge, so there were no white students. Mary ran a day school for the children and a night school for adults. School was held in a run-down old building where Mary and her students froze in the winter and broiled in the summer.

Her students were eager to learn, but often could not pay the small monthly school fees. Mary, however, struggled to pay the bills until the American Missionary Association hired her—at half pay—as the teacher in the school she herself had started.

## NOTES OF CANADA WEST

Myths and lies were circulating in the United States about life in Canada West. Mary, who wanted more American blacks to immigrate to Canada West, researched and wrote a forty four page booklet for black Americans called *Notes of Canada West*. Published in 1852, the inexpensive booklet was packed with useful information about life in Canada West. Included in the booklet was a discussion of the strengths and weaknesses of the different black settlements in Canada West.

## REFUGEE HOME SOCIETY

Mary's *Notes of Canada West* criticized the Refugee Home Society which was a local organization started by Henry Bibb and Mary's employers, the American Missionary Association. The Society was supposed to help fugitive slaves by encouraging them to buy small farms in a segregated black community.

**An early farm near Chatham, Canada West. Chatham had a large black population when Mary moved the headquarters of *The Provincial Freeman* there in 1855.**

All her life Mary believed that independence and self-respect were important qualities for her race. She argued there was no need for the Refugee Home Society because the black immigrants were able to work hard and do as well in their new country as any other group of immigrants.

Mary and other members of the black community were also irritated and embarrassed when Henry Bibb and members of the American Missionary Society went to the United States on money-gathering tours for the Refugee Home Society. Many agreed with Mary that the continual begging for the black refugees in Canada West was not needed and made them appear to be a community of beggars.

As well, in spite of all the money gathered on the tours, few black families ever lived on the Refugee Home Society farms. The charming Henry Bibb, however, mysteriously became richer and richer.

**Mary returned to the United States, but other members of the black community remained in Canada. The above photograph was taken around 1900 in Toronto, Ontario.**

Because she spoke out about the problems, the American Missionary Association fired Mary from her teaching position in Windsor. Rather than deal with the problems in their Refugee Home Society, the American Missionary Association took the easy way out and got rid of Mary— the messenger who had brought them the unpleasant news.

Mary, however, was well aware of the power of the press. Henry Bibb had used his own newspaper *The Voice of the Fugitive* to promote the Refugee Home Society and to attack any who dared to question or criticize the Society or Henry Bibb.

Mary, who never turned her back on a fight, decided the black community needed another newspaper.

## THE PROVINCIAL FREEMAN

Mary knew there would not be much support for a paper openly run by a woman. When, therefore, the *Provincial Freeman* began in the spring of 1853, the newspaper listed Samuel Ward as its editor. Samuel Ward was a Presbyterian minister who had been born into slavery but now lived in

**The Black Community in Canada: Graduation Photograph**

Toronto. He was a talented speaker and spent most of his time on speaking tours fighting for the abolition of slavery. Ward never edited the *Provincial Freeman*, however Mary hoped his famous name would help sell the newspaper. It was Mary Shadd who established and edited the weekly newspaper—the first black woman to do so in North America.

The *Provincial Freeman* was a lively paper that covered all aspects of black life in Canada with special attention paid to the problems of racial discrimination. The paper also took notice of the growing women's rights movement and commented upon the importance of women and their hard work. Lucretia Mott, the quiet, gentle Quaker abolitionist who began the women's movement in North America, gave several generous donations to the *Provincial Freeman* over the years.

## ON THE ROAD

Mary spent much of her time trying to raise enough money to keep the *Provincial Freeman* in business. At a time when it was unusual for women to speak in public, Mary repeatedly went on lecture tours throughout the United States speaking out against slavery, encouraging black immigration to Canada and seeking financial support for her paper. The trips were often unpleasant, for Mary had very little money and had to travel as cheaply as possible. As well, even in the Northern States, black travelers could expect insults and second-rate treatment in hotels, restaurants, boats and stage coaches.

## A MAN'S JOB

In 1854 Mary moved the paper's headquarters to Toronto, Canada West, where there was a black population of over one thousand people. Samuel Ward's name was removed from the newspaper and the name M. A. Shadd appeared as editor. Her sister Amelia ran the paper when Mary was away on her exhausting fund-raising lecture tours through Canada West and the northern states. Readers assumed that M. A. Shadd was a man, but when Mary finally explained in print that the editor of the *Provincial Freeman* was a woman, there was a huge outcry. There was so much public outrage over a woman doing "a man's job" that Mary was afraid readers would stop buying the paper and the last black paper in Canada would have to close.

Discouraged and angered by public reaction, Mary nonetheless found a male editor for her paper. The new editor, Reverend William Newman, lived in Dawn, a black community near Chatham, Canada West. In 1855, Mary moved the headquarters of the *Provincial Freeman* to Chatham.

The move made sense for a number of reasons. At that time there was a black population of over two thousand people in the Chatham area, and Mary believed the *Provincial Freeman* would attract much local advertising. As well, Mary's parents and many of her sisters and brothers had immigrated to Canada and now lived in the black community of Buxton, which was also close to Chatham. While in Chatham, Mary rescued a young escaped slave from slave catchers illegally at work in Canada West.

## RECOGNITION AND MARRIAGE

During one of her lecture tours for the paper, the clever and beautiful Mary Shadd dazzled Philadelphia with her speaking and debating skills. A benefit was held in that city to honour Mary's years of hard work and achievement in the black rights movement.

In 1856 Mary married Thomas Cary who was a hard working member of the black community. Five days after the wedding Mary was again lecturing and travelling to raise funds for the *Provincial Freeman*. In spite of Mary's hard work, a depression swept across Canada West and the hard times forced Mary to stop publishing her paper in 1857.

Thomas Cary died in 1861 leaving Mary with a young daughter and son.

## BACK TO THE USA

The American Civil War ended in 1865 and slavery was finally illegal in the United States. Mary knew a huge task lay ahead educating the millions of newly freed slaves. She returned to the United States where she taught school for many years and then, at the age of sixty, became a lawyer.

In 1865 the United States gave the vote to black men but refused to give the vote to women. Mary used her energy and skills to work for the American women's rights movement but did not live to see women win the vote.

The courageous Mary Shadd Cary, a woman who never turned away from a fight, died quietly at the age of seventy.


Further Suggested Reading:

Bearden, Jim and Linda Jean Butler. *Shadd*. Toronto: NC Press Limited, 1977.

**Dr Emily Jennings Stowe.  Emily attended the Toronto School of Medicine in 1870.  The male medical students scrawled so many foul and hideous comments on the classroom walls that they had to be whitewashed four times in one term.**

# CHAPTER 10

## CANADA'S FIRST WOMAN DOCTOR

# DR EMILY JENNINGS STOWE

## (1831-1903)

**I will make it the business of my life to see that the doors will be open, that women may have the same opportunities as men.**

**—Dr Emily Jennings Stowe**

*Emily Stowe and Jennie Trout paused outside the closed door. What new horror would be waiting inside today, they wondered. No doubt they would find gruesome objects, such as severed arms or hands, left on their chairs as a sick joke. They would probably see disgusting pictures and messages on the blackboards and walls scrawled there by the men students and teachers.*

*Emily and Jennie knew, however, that they must continue to hide their feelings of shock and disgust. If they did not, the men would say women were weak and did not belong in the class.*

*The women smiled bravely at each other, then opened the door. Another terrible day at Medical School was about to begin.*

## MEN AND WOMEN ARE EQUAL

Emily Jennings, the eldest of six girls, was born in 1831 in the pioneer village of Norwich, Canada West (now Ontario). Her parents, Hannah and Solomon Jennings, had once been members of a Christian religious group called The Society of Friends or Quakers. The Quakers believed that men and women were equal and should share rights and responsibilities equally—unusual ideas for the 1800s. Emily and her sisters were raised to believe in their own abilities and to believe women could do whatever men could do.

## TEACHER AND PRINCIPAL

When Emily was fifteen, she began teaching in Norwich's one-room school. Emily, however, wanted to further her education. When she was in her twenties, she applied to study at the University of Toronto. The

University turned her application down because women were not allowed to attend university.

Emily was disappointed but went to teachers' college in Toronto, instead. Since 1850, children in Canada West (now Ontario) had the right to free schooling. This caused a sudden demand for teachers, both men and women. With a certificate from teachers' college, Emily knew she could get a better teaching position and higher pay.

Emily did so well at teachers' college that she became the public school principal in Brantford, Canada West. Emily was the first woman principal in Canada.

In 1856, at age twenty-five, Emily married John Stowe, a carriage-maker, who lived in the nearby town of Mount Pleasant. Few employers would allow a married woman to hold a job. Emily, therefore, gave up her job as school principal in order to become a wife.

## HALF PAY

Emily, John, and their three children, lived happy, busy lives until illness struck the family. John became ill with tuberculosis, a deadly disease of the lungs, and was sent to a special hospital to recover. With John ill, his carriage business ended. Suddenly there was no money to pay the family's ordinary bills, let alone John's expensive hospital bills.

Emily had no choice but to return to teaching in order to support her family. She was fortunate to obtain a teaching job at a private school in Mount Pleasant, but it was difficult for the family to manage on her low salary.

Women teachers were paid less than half of what men teachers received, even if the women had the same education and taught the same number of grades and subjects.

The excuse for such low pay was that men teachers usually had a family to support but women would only teach until they married. Once they were married, it was argued, their husbands would support them. In other words, the amount of money a teacher earned was based on the person's need for money, not on the person's education or ability to teach.

This weak excuse ignored reality. Some women teachers never married and some men teachers did not have a family to support. As well, some women teachers did have a family to support because their husbands were seriously ill or dead. Women teachers like Emily needed more money to support a family, but, because they were women, they were still paid half of what a man would receive for the same job.

Why then, were women willing to teach? In the 1800s there were many types of jobs open to men, but teaching was one of the few respectable jobs open to women. The many women who had to earn a living were forced to accept the lower rate of pay or lose the job—and starve.

## TOO DELICATE

While John was ill, Emily came to a shocking decision—she would become a doctor. She applied to the University of Toronto medical school and was turned down because she was a woman.

Emily was disappointed, but not surprised. Before the 1800s, healing, especially within the home and in rural communities, was often a woman's job. By the 1800s, however, attitudes had changed and women were, for the most part, not allowed to become doctors. Queen Victoria reigned from 1837 to 1901, and during this period women were expected to behave in a "proper" manner. It was not proper for women to discuss or even know much about the human body, pregnancy or childbirth. Doctors, of course, had to know about the human body. Some people felt no proper woman could be interested in a career that studied the human body.

The men who ran the university medical schools also argued that women were too delicate and did not have the physical strength to be doctors. These men ignored the fact that bearing children and running a household in the 1800s with no electricity or running water in the home took a great deal of physical strength. As well, many women worked in the fields, worked in mines and worked in factory sweat shops—all of which took more physical strength than the work of a doctor.

Emily knew, however, there was a great need for women doctors. The need for proper women to be timid about the human body also meant many women were too shy to discuss their health problems with a man—even if the man was a doctor. As a result, women were suffering and dying needlessly.

In the United States, women were also kept out of colleges and universities. However, a few medical colleges for women had been set up. Emily wanted to save women's lives and decided she would study medicine even if she had to leave her own country to do so. She saved enough money to study at the New York Medical College for Women while her sister stayed with the children.

Emily missed her family, but graduated and became a doctor in 1867—the same year as Canada's Confederation. The Stowes moved to Toronto where Emily became the first Canadian woman doctor to practice medicine in Canada.

## PROBLEMS AHEAD

Emily soon became a busy doctor, for many women preferred to be treated by another woman. However, shortly after she graduated, a law was passed that said all doctors who had trained in the United States must attend one term of lectures at an Ontario medical school and take a set of examinations before they could earn their license to practice medicine in Ontario. The University of Toronto medical school still refused to let a woman attend lectures so Emily was forced to practice without her medical license.

After Emily had applied many times, the University of Toronto grudgingly allowed Emily, and a young woman by the name of Jennie Trout, to attend medical lectures for one term. The women were told, however, they were not to complain about anything.

The teachers and male medical students were dreadful to the two women. They tried to stop Emily and Jennie from attending classes by leaving filth and hideous objects on the women's chairs, by deliberately talking about obscene topics, and by scribbling disgusting words and pictures on the walls and blackboards. The two women, however, refused to be frightened away and finished the term successfully.

Emily's husband John recovered from tuberculosis, and Emily supported him while he studied dentistry. John became a dentist in 1878, and Emily and John practiced together in Toronto.

## TOO DELICATE TO VOTE

Emily could have devoted the rest of her life to her family and her busy practice, but she did not. Emily was keenly aware that, as a woman, she did not have the same rights as a man, and this too, she wanted to change.

By law, after a woman married, everything she owned belonged to her husband. As well, during marriage the wages she earned and what-ever she inherited would also belong to her husband. The husband also had total control over the children of the marriage. He could give them up for adoption, send them out to work at a young age, decide whether or not to educate them, decide their religion, and decide who would raise them if he should die. The mother had no legal rights in any of these matters.

As a doctor, Emily saw many examples of women and children who suffered as a result of these unfair laws. She decided the law treated women so harshly because women were not allowed to vote. Again, women were told they were too delicate to make important decisions and

# TOO DELICATE TO VOTE

▲
Chopping
firewood

At work in
a Quebec
copper
mine

# TOO DELICATE TO VOTE

**Wash day on the prairies**

**Bringing home supper**

were therefore too delicate to vote in elections. Without votes, women were powerless to bring about change. Once women had the vote, however, Emily believed women would elect people who promised to change the unfair laws.

In 1877 Emily organized a group which worked for women's rights. It was the first of its kind in Canada. *Suffrage* means the right to vote at elections, and Emily's group was later called the Toronto Women's Suffrage Association. In spite of her busy life, Emily travelled all over Ontario lecturing and explaining why women should have the vote. Some women showed up just to see what a woman doctor looked like. The women then stayed to listen with interest as Emily talked about women's rights and the need for change.

## DOORS TO OPEN

Under Emily's leadership the Toronto Women's Suffrage Association helped improve working conditions for women factory workers and sales clerks. Emily also wanted women to have the right to attend university. In 1884 the Women's Suffrage Association forced the University of Toronto to allow women to attend its arts courses.

The University of Toronto still refused to let women attend its medical school. Emily, however, wanted Canadian women to be able to study medicine in Canada, and she worked and campaigned until the Ontario Medical College for Women opened in Toronto in 1883.

Also in 1883, Emily's daughter, Augusta, became the first woman to receive a degree in medicine in Canada. Augusta married another doctor in her class at medical school and became Dr Augusta Stowe-Gullen. She too worked hard as a medical doctor, yet made time to work with her mother for women's rights.

## THE POWER OF LAUGHTER

Sometimes Emily and the other women in the suffrage movement used humour to advance the cause of women's rights. In 1896 the Women's Suffrage Association put on a mock Parliament. Women played the roles of various members of Parliament just as if women had always been in power. Emily and her daughter Augusta played the part of cabinet ministers.

The audience watched as a group of men came to the mock Parliament and begged for a law that would give men the right to vote. The women, however, cleverly handed back the type of answers women had so often received when they asked for the vote. The women claimed that giving men the vote would mean that soon men would want to wear women's clothes and try to do women's jobs! They also pointed out that men were designed to do the heavy work and should leave the running of the country to the women.

The audience enjoyed the humour and the mock Parliament was a success. Many left that evening wondering why women did not have the vote.

## A FIGHTER TO THE END

Even when Emily retired as a doctor at age sixty-two, she continued to work for women's rights—lecturing, writing letters and attending meetings. She died in 1903 at the age of seventy-one—before women won the vote. The Ontario women's suffrage movement, however, continued to work until Ontario women won the vote in 1917.

As well, thanks largely to Emily's efforts, during her lifetime women won the right to attend university and to attend their own medical school. At the time of Emily's death there were over 120 women doctors in Canada; forty years earlier there had been none.

Today, many of the rights Canadian women now take for granted, are possible because of the efforts of Dr Emily Jennings Stowe.

Further Suggested Reading:

Ray, Janet. *Emily Stowe*. Toronto: Fitzhenry & Whiteside Limited, 1978.

McCallum, Margaret. *Emily Stowe*. Toronto: Grolier Limited, 1989.

# CHAPTER 11

## POET

# PAULINE JOHNSON

## (1861 - 1913)

**Never let anyone call me a white woman . . . I am Indian and my aim, my joy and my pride is to sing the glories of my own people.**
**—Pauline Johnson**

*Hoots and catcalls greeted the woman as she walked out onto the platform. The jeers and insults from the crowd had already forced the two previous performers to leave the stage in tears.*

*Pauline Johnson, however, knew how to control an audience. She looked up at the balcony where the young troublemakers were sitting and began to speak. "When I see a crowd of boys having a good time in the balcony, I am always sorry . . . "The boys, expecting a scolding, drowned out the rest of her words with boos and loud groans. When the noise died down, Pauline continued in her strong, clear voice. "Yes, I am sorry I am not up there with them!"*

*The audience howled with laughter and broke into loud applause. The evening's ugly mood had changed and there were no more interruptions.*

## AN IMPORTANT FAMILY

Emily Pauline Johnson was born on the Six Nations Reserve near Brantford, Ontario, on 10 March 1861. She was a beautiful child, with gray eyes and wavy, brown hair. Pauline was proud to be a member of one of Canada's First Nations.

Pauline's father, George Henry Martin Johnson, was a Mohawk— one of the nations belonging to the Iroquois Confederacy or Six Nations. Her great-grandfather, Jacob Johnson, had been the godson of Molly Brant's husband, Sir William Johnson. Jacob Johnson had taken the last name Johnson when he joined the Anglican faith. After the defeat of Britain and her allies in the American Revolution, Pauline's great-grandparents moved with the famous Mohawk leader, Joseph Brant, to a large piece of land, later known as the Six Nations Reserve.

Pauline Johnson in her buckskin costume

Pauline's grandfather, John "Smoke" Johnson, was a hero of the War of 1812. Like Laura Secord's husband, James Secord, Smoke Johnson had served with General Isaac Brock at the famous Battle of Queenston Heights. He had also fought at other battles including the Battle of Beaver Dams, the battle where the Americans were soundly beaten with the help of information supplied by Laura Secord.

Pauline's Mohawk grandmother, Helen Martin Johnson, was head of the Mohawk Clan Mothers, a powerful group of Iroquois women who chose and trained the peace chief.

Pauline's father, George Johnson, was a well-educated man who spoke and read English, French, German as well as the six languages of the Six Nations. When he announced he was going to marry Emily Susanna Howells, the English sister-in-law of the Anglican missionary who lived on the Six Nations Reserve, he deeply shocked and disappointed his parents. The Iroquois traced their family line through their mothers, not their fathers, and it was important for an Iroquois son to marry a woman from a high-ranking Iroquois family.

The family of Emily Susanna Howells was also against the marriage, but the couple married in spite of all the opposition. Their marriage was a happy one, and George Johnson was appointed chief of his nation. George was well-to-do and built a beautiful mansion  called Chiefswood on the Six Nations Reserve for his English bride.

## LIFE AT CHIEFSWOOD

Pauline grew up in an elegant home where the dining room table was formally set at every meal with crisp, white linen, fine china and silver cutlery. Chiefswood had luxuries such as a piano and a library filled with classics by English poets and writers. Pauline was allowed to read as much as she wanted and was encouraged by her mother in her love of poetry.

Many were eager to visit Chiefswood, and the Johnsons entertained British aristocrats, scholars, famous writers and actors from around the world. Pauline's gracious style of life at Chiefswood allowed her to feel at ease when, years later, she mingled with the rich and famous in London, England.

## EDUCATION

Pauline studied at home for two years with a governess, then attended school on the reserve and later went to high school in Brantford. The Johnson children, however, were brought up to think of themselves as

Mohawks, and Pauline's real education came from her grandfather, Smoke Johnson. Pauline dearly loved her grandfather who was a famous Iroquois speaker. He taught her about the history and traditions of the Mohawk people and gave her a deep sense of pride in her native culture.

Pauline was an expert canoeist and spent many happy hours on the Grand River that flowed past her home. She loved nature and in her canoe Pauline fully enjoyed the world and its beauty.

## GOOD-BYE TO ALL THAT

After her schooling ended, Pauline lived the life of a well-to-do young lady. She spent her time attending parties, acting in plays, writing poetry and visiting friends. With the death of her father, however, Pauline's happy, sheltered life at Chiefswood ended.

For many years Chief George Johnson had courageously fought against white traders who tried to trade cheap liquor for valuable timber growing on the Six Nations Reserve. Chief Johnson received two savage beatings from his white enemies which damaged his health and led to his early death in 1884.

After Pauline's father died, the Johnson family had very little money. Chiefswood was closed up, and Pauline rented an apartment in Brantford with her mother and sister. Her two older brothers had jobs in other cities, but Pauline and her sister Eva now had to find a way to earn a living. There were few jobs open to young ladies in the late 1880s, but Eva was able to find an office job in Brantford. Pauline, now twenty-three, hoped to earn money by writing and selling her poetry.

## POETRY AND POVERTY

Pauline, who had written poems all her life, began to sell her poems to magazines. She built a good reputation for herself but found it difficult to make a living as a poet. Pauline was paid only three dollars for her best known poem, *Song My Paddle Sings*. Another poem that was featured on a magazine cover brought in only seventy-five cents! In her entire lifetime Pauline made no more than five hundred dollars from her poems.

In 1892, when Pauline was thirty-one, she was invited to take part in a concert by reading from her work. Pauline thrilled the audience when she recited her poem *A Cry From An Indian Wife*. They applauded loudly and demanded she recite another poem. It was obvious that Pauline was a gifted speaker who could deeply move an audience. It was also obvious that Pauline was talented enough to make a living by giving recitals.

▲

The First Children:
A Makah girl.
Pauline tried to
visit other First
Nations when she
was on tour.

The First Children:
A Peigan girl in
front of her play
lodge.

**The First Children:  A Clayoquot child**

In 1893, Pauline began a new career. She made a striking costume out of buckskin and became a platform entertainer.

## A PLATFORM ENTERTAINER

In the late 1800s, radio, movies and television had not been invented. Most communities depended upon touring performers for entertainment. The men and women who were platform entertainers sang, or recited, or put on magic shows, or performed short selections from famous plays. Performances took place in schools, tents, saloons and church halls—wherever an audience could gather.

Although Pauline's family disapproved of platform entertainers, Pauline began recital tours in 1893 and gave 125 recitals in 50 different communities. The tours took her through Ontario, the Maritimes and the Eastern United States.

Pauline loved reciting and her audiences loved her in return. Her speaking skills, probably inherited or learned from her Mohawk grandfather, together with her charm, humour and high spirits made a Pauline Johnson concert an unforgettable event.

## LONDON

By the summer of 1894, Pauline earned enough money from her concerts to travel to London, England. She hoped to find a London publisher for her poems. Because of her reputation as a poet, Pauline arrived in London with letters of introduction from the governor general of Canada, the lieutenant governor of Ontario and the president of the University of Toronto.

While in England, Pauline was much in demand at the glittering parties of the great London hostesses. Pauline dressed in native costume and often recited her poetry for the other guests. Raised to have the proper, formal manners of a Victorian lady, she easily mingled with other distinguished party guests. Some of the guests had visited Chiefswood years earlier.

Pauline was successful in finding a publisher and her first book of poems, entitled *The White Wampum*, was published in England in 1895.

## MORE CONCERTS

Although *The White Wampum* received good reviews, Pauline did not make enough money from book sales to keep poverty from the door. In 1895, Pauline returned to the life of a platform entertainer. For the next fourteen years Pauline crossed back and forth across Canada and the

A Squamish woman. The Squamish once occupied almost all of the area that is now Vancouver, British Columbia.

mid-western United States on a series of exhausting tours. She visited other First Nations during her travels and fought against the narrow, incorrect views many whites held about native people.

Automobiles were still rare so Pauline traveled by train, and when there was no train, by horse and wagon. Her fame spread and Pauline became the leading platform entertainer in Canada. Her concerts were often sold out, but her life on the road was difficult. The beds were often hard, the rooms unheated and the food poor. Just getting from one performance to another took much of her energy and Pauline had little time on the road to relax or read or write. Yet in each little town or village Pauline gave an unforgettable performance, thrilling audiences with fiery ballads then soothing them with gentle poems about nature's beauty. Audiences responded with love and admiration.

Pauline's many travels taught her to love Canada with a passion and she wanted her audiences to share her love of country. In some remote communities Pauline was the first entertainer to arrive in many years, and people rode over one hundred kilometres to hear her recite. She told the tiny, far-flung communities she visited about the First Nations and about the vast and magnificent country of Canada.

Her second book of poetry, *Canadian Born*, was published in 1903. Later both poetry books were combined and published in a book called *Flint and Feather*.

## HER LAST WORK

During her seventeen years of concert-giving, Pauline somehow found time to write short stories and articles for a number of Canadian and British publications. She made more money with prose than with poetry and when, exhausted, she retired from concert-giving in 1909, Pauline decided to earn her living as a writer.

She settled in Vancouver, British Columbia, a city she had always loved, and spent time listening to the stories of the Squamish chief, Joe Capilano. Pauline carefully wrote down the ancient Squamish stories she had heard from Chief Capilano. The stories were first published as a series of articles in a Vancouver newspaper.

As Pauline worked on the Squamish stories she grew weaker and weaker until she discovered in 1911 that she had breast cancer. Pauline was a generous person and had often given money to help others. Now she had little money left and was too sick to support herself with her writing.

Her friends in Vancouver knew Pauline would not accept charity so they arranged for her beautiful Squamish stories to be published in book form. Over twelve thousand copies of *Legends of Vancouver* were sold. The book profits allowed Pauline to support herself during her long, painful illness.

Pauline died of breast cancer at age fifty-two, and Canadians everywhere mourned the loss. The city of Vancouver flew its flags at half-mast, and huge crowds attended the funeral of this talented poet who had thrilled so many audiences.

Pauline's ashes were buried in Vancouver's beautiful Stanley Park on 10 March 1913.

Further Suggested Reading:

Willowby, Brenda. *Pauline Johnson*. Toronto: Grolier Limited, 1991.

Norcross, Blanche. *Pioneers Every One*. Burns & MacEachern Limited, 1979.

# CHAPTER 12

## HIGH SOCIETY SOURDOUGH

# MARTHA MUNGER BLACK

## —————— (1866 - 1957) ——————

**I liked the life, the vigorous challenge of it—the work and play of it.**
**—Martha Munger Black**

*Martha knew there was no turning back. The pretty, thirty-two-year-old woman staggered along in the unbroken line of filthy, sweating, half-starved men. Only a few months ago she had been a pampered member of high society, but now she was just another gold seeker, struggling up a narrow, slippery mountain trail to the never-ending sound of groans, curses and cracking whips.*

*Dogs and horses, carrying packs or pulling sleighs along the mountain trail, lurched forward with their heavy burdens. Some overloaded pack horses slipped and fell off the narrow path. Martha heard their wild screams of terror as the horses plunged to their death on the rocks far below.*

*"Don't look down! Don't look down!" the others warned.*

### AMERICAN SOCIALITE

Martha Munger was born in Chicago, Illinois, in 1866, the only daughter of a well-to-do businessman. She married William Purdy who came from another wealthy and respected Chicago family. Martha and William had two sons, and for ten years Martha lived a high society life of parties and volunteer work. She was, however, bored and unhappy.

### GOLD IN THE KLONDIKE!

In 1897, news came out of Canada that gold had been discovered on the Klondike River in Canada's Yukon Territory. The Klondike Gold Rush was on and Martha's life changed forever.

Like thousands of others, both Martha's husband and her brother George, caught gold fever and decided to seek their fortunes in Canada. The trip, however, would be long and dangerous. First they would have to take the boat up the west coast to Dyea, Alaska, then travel by foot over the Rocky Mountains through the dreaded Chilkoot Pass. After they crossed Chilkoot Pass, they would then be in the Yukon Territory and would have to travel down rivers and lakes to Dawson City, where the Yukon and Klondike rivers met.

Martha longed for adventure and insisted on going too. In 1898 the Purdys left their two sons with Martha's parents and set off with Martha's brother George to seek gold. Once on the west coast, however, Martha's husband changed his mind. The trip was too dangerous, William decided, and he no longer wished to go. He suggested Martha return to her parents until he decided what he wanted to do.

Martha was furious! She had already bought her boat ticket and did not want to return to Chicago's dull society life. Although feeling ill in the early stages of pregnancy, she decided to travel to the Klondike with her brother George, as planned. She told William Purdy that she never wanted to see him again—and she never did.

## THE UTOPIA

In June of 1898, Martha and her travelling companions left Seattle on the ship *Utopia*. Crowded boats set sail every hour loaded down with people, sleds, carts, horses, cattle, oxen and food supplies—all heading for the Yukon. The seven-day, twenty-two-thousand-kilometre sea voyage wound around the many coastal islands of British Columbia.

The word *utopia* means "perfect place" but for Martha, the dirty, overloaded, old steamer she was travelling on was far from perfect. The captain of the ship was usually drunk and wild drinking and gambling parties went on day and night. Men slept on the saloon floor and in every available corner of the overloaded ship. Martha was forced to share her small room with three others—a gambler and his companion and an unusual woman by the name of Birdie.

At first proper, high-society Martha was shocked by the idea of sharing her room with strangers, but she soon learned to enjoy her odd roommates. The gambler brought her coffee every morning, and Birdie shared with Martha expensive oranges and apples from her own private supplies.

The weather was perfect, the food good and the wild mountain scenery exciting. After travelling north for two days they found them-selves in "the land of the midnight sun." The June days lengthened until it was never truly dark; there were only a few hours of twilight before the sun rose in the sky again.

**Sheep Camp in 1898, where gold seekers prepared for the terrible climb up Chilkoot Pass. The tiny black dots are people struggling up the Golden Steps of Chilkoot Pass.**

Martha and her brother unloaded at Dyea, Alaska, which was the closest port to the famous Chilkoot Pass. Dyea was a city of tents, full of thousands of other gold seekers preparing to climb the Rocky Mountains.

## THE GOLD TRAIL

On 12 July 1898 Martha and her brother took their place in the line of people and animals that moved from Dyea along the ninety-two-kilometre trail over Chilkoot Pass and down to Lake Bennett. In front and

**113**

behind Martha were men carrying thirty to forty kilograms of supplies on their backs. There were also pack horses, oxen and driving dogs harnessed to carts all straining under their loads. Sadly, of the hundreds of horses that started out, probably none made it alive over Chilkoot Pass. The last section of the trail was almost straight up "The Golden Steps"—narrow, slippery steps chopped out of solid ice that were impossible for dogs, let alone horses, to climb.

Martha described the mountain path as "a trail of heartbreak and dead hopes." On every side were dozens of rotting carcasses of horses which had slipped and fallen down the mountainside. As the trail grew steeper, and narrower, it was littered with more and more clothes, trunks and other items tossed behind by earlier gold seekers. At some points the mountain trail became so narrow that Martha could only move forward by placing one foot carefully in front of the other.

Martha and her party were able to travel light because they hired men called packers to carry their supplies over the trail for them. Most gold seekers, however, could not afford this luxury and had to carry their food and other supplies with them on their backs.

## MUSH ON!

The first night on the trail was spent in a shack in Sheep Camp on the edge of the tree line. The place was full of tired, sweating men crammed into tiny shacks and tents where one meal cost two days' wages, and the chance to sleep on the floor cost a small fortune. High above the camp could be seen a thin, unbroken black line crawling almost straight up a naked wall of ice and snow. These were gold seekers ahead of them on the last nine kilometre climb to the top of Chilkoot Pass. Gold seekers resting in Sheep Camp knew that soon, they too would be a tiny black speck high up on that treacherous trail.

The next day Martha and her brother again took their place in line and began the climb. The hot July sun melted the snow and made the trail icy, but the long line of gold seekers pushed on. "Mush on!" from the French word *marchons*, meaning "push on," was the cry of the North. Those who staggered off the narrow trail to rest, might wait for hours until there was a space for them to crawl back in line.

Martha, dressed in the impractical women's clothing of the time, struggled along the trail. Her tight, boned corsets made breathing difficult and she had to yank up her heavy, ankle-length skirts and full silk bloomers every step of the way. Near the top she slipped off the icy trail and slashed her leg on a rock, but managed to continue the climb. Aching

**The miners and prospectors of the Yukon treated Martha with kindness and respect. Martha's cabin became a popular place where the lonely men could sing, play the guitar and talk about their families back home.**

and bone-weary, Martha finally made it to the top of Chilkoot Pass and crossed into Canadian territory.

She admired the sturdy North West Mounted Police who were the law in the Yukon. They guarded the Canadian border at the top of the Chilkoot Pass and turned back anyone who did not have a year's supplies with them. The Mounties also policed the Yukon with an iron hand. Unlike parts of Alaska where robberies and murders occurred frequently, those living in the Yukon rarely bothered to even lock their doors. Yukoners knew the Mounties would not tolerate theft or violent crime.

## DAWSON CITY

The trip down from Chilkoot Pass was, if anything, more difficult. Already exhausted, Martha's shaky legs and aching feet often tripped over trees roots and jagged rocks along the trail which ended at Lake Bennett. Cooking for the others, Martha quickly learned to make sourdough—the fluffy bread made without yeast which the Klondike Gold Rush made famous around the world.

For twelve days Martha's group sailed in a tiny boat through northern lakes and rivers. Along the way they stopped at a Mounted Police post where they were told 18,000 men had already passed that way, but only 630 women.

When they sailed in to Dawson City in August, they found it was another crowded city of dirty tents and one-room shacks. However, by 1898 it also bulged with hastily built saloons, theatres, dance halls, hotels and restaurants—all ready to help those who struck it rich, spend their gold. In the dance halls lonely but newly rich men could drink, gamble and watch women with names like Ping Pong, Spanish Jeanette, Lime Juice Lil (she refused to drink liquor) and Sweet Marie dance and sing. One of the most famous of these dancers, Diamond Tooth Gertie later married a leading Dawson City lawyer.

**As part of the mining process, stream water was sent through wooden sluice-boxes that held soil dug from the mine. The running water washed away the soil and left the heavier gold dust and nuggets behind.**

Women in the Yukon made their living in a variety of ways. In spite of the high prices, some miners and prospectors ate their meals at Mary's Coffee House. In the summer, Mary grew lettuce on the roof of the building.

Miner's cabins were small, with dirt floors and built-in bunks. Little "Klondyke stoves," fueled with wood, kept the cabins snug in the long Arctic winters.

# LIFE IN THE YUKON

Aware of the malaria, typhoid fever and smallpox that sometimes broke out in Dawson City, Martha and her brother and the four other men in her group built a small log cabin up on a hill just outside the city. They made furniture out of tree trunks, twigs and packing cases. Martha staked a claim by pounding wooden stakes into a certain piece of land and then buying the rights to mine it.

By the last week of October it was winter in the Yukon. Because of high prices, winter also meant six months of going without milk, butter or sugar. The sun would only creep above the horizon for a few hours and then the land was plunged back into another twenty-two hours of Arctic darkness. Some days the temperature fell to seventy below zero and the dishwater, when thrown out the back door, froze before it fell to the ground! For Martha, the winter of 1898 also meant her baby would soon be born. She made baby clothes and diapers out of cloth napkins and tablecloths.

Unable to afford a doctor, she was alone in the cabin when she gave birth to her third son in January 1899. Word of the birth spread and miners from all over, lonely for their own children, often stopped by with generous gifts "for the kid and his ma." The big, rough, shaggy-looking men loved to hold and play with the baby. Even bath time became a daily show as delighted miners crammed into the tiny cabin to watch the baby splash about.

# RETURN OF THE SOURDOUGH

When springtime arrived in 1899, Martha became an official Sourdough— someone who had spent a winter in the Yukon and watched the Yukon River freeze and then thaw the next spring.

By this time a railway had been built through the Rocky Mountains, so travel in and out of the Yukon was easier. Martha took her new son to her parent's luxurious home in Kansas, but felt restless and useless away from the North. She gladly returned to the Yukon where her claims, worked for her by her brother George, had yielded gold.

Martha then formed a gold mining partnership with two other men. She cooked for their mining camp of sixteen men, rising at 5:00 am to start the meals. She divorced William Purdy and made sure each of her sons spent time living with her in the Yukon. Martha also ran a successful sawmill business in Dawson City. Her business did so well that she was able to live well and buy the latest fashions, including beautiful gowns imported from Paris, France.

## GOOD TIMES IN THE YUKON

The men and women of the Klondike loved to hold dances and annual balls, especially during the long, dreary winter months. The hope of finding adventure and gold had brought people from all walks of life and from many different countries. As a result, the Dawson City orchestras were made up of talented musicians from all over the world. On the dance floor, men in tuxedos and Mounties in their handsome scarlet uniforms danced to lovely music with women dressed in expensive French ball gowns. At the end of the dance, as the sled dogs howled, the handsomely dressed men and women trudged back through the Arctic winter to their rough log cabins.

## MARTHA BLACK, MEMBER OF PARLIAMENT

Eventually Martha married George Black, a Yukon lawyer and Sourdough who was originally from the province of New Brunswick. George was appointed Commissioner of Yukon Territory and was elected Yukon's member of Parliament for many years.

Martha spent much of World War I in London, England, to be close to her husband and the young men of the Yukon Infantry Company who were under her husband's command. Martha, who spent much of this time doing volunteer work for the war effort, found the damp cold of England far more unbearable than the Yukon's arctic winters.

Martha never lost her love of the North and in 1935, at the age of sixty-nine, she was elected member of Parliament for Yukon Territory. She was the second woman to be elected to Canada's House of Commons in Ottawa. Her life continued to be full and exciting to the very end. Martha Munger Black, the high society Sourdough, died in her beloved Yukon at the age of ninety-one.

Further suggested reading:

Black, Martha Louise. *My Seventy Years* Toronto: Thomas Nelson and Sons Ltd., 1938.

Johnston, Jean. *Wilderness Women*. Toronto: Peter Martin Associates Limited, 1976.

# CHAPTER 13

## FIRST WOMAN MAGISTRATE IN THE BRITISH EMPIRE

# EMILY FERGUSON MURPHY

## —————— (1868 - 1933) ——————

**The world loves a peaceful man, but gives way to a strenuous kicker.**

**—Emily Ferguson Murphy**

*Emily cautiously watched the lawyer rise from his seat in the courtroom. It was her first day as a judge, but she knew this particular lawyer was a cunning one.*

*"I object," said the lawyer, "to a woman judge. The law clearly states a judge must be 'a person' and, by law, a woman is not 'a person'," he finished in triumph.*

*If the lawyer hoped he would stop the first woman judge in the British Empire, he was wrong. Emily Ferguson Murphy was a fighter. If some absurd law said that a woman was not "a person," then Emily would fight until that law was changed.*

### RAISED LIKE A BOY

Emily was born in 1868 in Cookstown, Ontario, into the wealthy and respectable Ferguson family. Sir John A. Macdonald, Canada's first Prime Minister, was a family friend and sometimes visited the Fergusons. Three of Emily's brothers became important lawyers and her other brother became a doctor, yet it was Emily who became the most famous member of this successful family.

Emily was given a strange upbringing for a young lady in the 1800s—she was expected to do whatever her brothers did—both the games and the chores. As a result, Emily had a busy, happy childhood fishing, playing cricket, and riding and grooming her pony.

At fifteen she attended Bishop Strachan School, a private school in Toronto for the daughters of the wealthy. While at school, young Emily met Arthur Murphy, a tall, blonde, good-looking college student who was studying to become an Anglican minister. Arthur was captivated by tiny, lively Emily Ferguson. "Hurry and grow up," Arthur told her on their first meeting, "so I can marry you."

Emily and Arthur were married in 1887 when Emily was nineteen. Full of common sense and good humour, Arthur would always be a loving and supportive husband for the high-spirited and strong-willed Emily Ferguson.

## JANEY CANUCK

As the minister's wife Emily learned skills she would use all her life. She spoke at meetings, set up women's work groups, and organized fund-raising projects.

The Murphy's and their three daughters (another daughter had died at nine months of age) sailed to England in 1898 so that Arthur could preach in England and Europe. Emily enjoyed the sightseeing, but she was shocked by the poverty and despair she saw in England's dirty, crowded cities.

A common nickname for a Canadian was "Johnny Canuck." Emily wrote a book about her travels in England and Europe and playfully called it *Impressions of Janey Canuck Abroad*. The book was published in 1901 and was a success in Great Britain and in Canada.

## A TIME OF DESPAIR

When the Murphy's returned to Toronto, Arthur became deadly ill with typhoid. As Arthur struggled for his life, the bills mounted. Emily looked after Arthur during the day and worked through the nights writing articles and book reviews for magazines. Her writing supported the family until Emily too, came down with typhoid.

Emily recovered, but as she struggled to regain her strength, her youngest daughter, age six, died of diphtheria. Emily and Arthur, still weak from their own illnesses, sank into deep despair. Arthur gave up church work, and the Murphys moved to Manitoba where they hoped, like thousands of others, to find fresh air and a fresh beginning.

## IMMIGRANTS IN THE MID-WEST

Emily wrote three books about her life in the western frontier: *Janey Canuck in the West*, *Open Trails*, and *Seeds of Pine*. All three were about Emily's adventures with interesting people and places. The books sold well and Janey Canuck became a household name.

The Murphys moved to Edmonton, Alberta, in 1907. At that time ten thousand people a month passed through Edmonton on their way to new

# THOSE WHO CAME TO CANADA

Russian Jews

Roumanians

**Laplanders**

**Chinese**

homes in the West. Immigrants from all over the world left behind poverty or religious persecution, hoping to find a better life.

Some Canadians felt that anyone who did not come from Great Britain was a foreigner and should not be made welcome. Emily did not agree. She defended the new immigrants in her Janey Canuck books as "coming Canadians" who were helping to build a new Canada. "On the streets . . ." she wrote, "there are people who smile at you in English but speak in Russian."

Emily admired the Doukabour immigrant women who did heavy work in the fields as well as the spinning, knitting, linen-making and food preparation. Emily envied the loose, comfortable clothing of the Doukabour women compared to the painfully tight corsets made with pieces of bone and steel which fashion forced ladies to wear. The bodies of Doukabour women were not, Emily muttered, locked away in "jails of bones and steels."

## SOCIAL REFORM

Emily Murphy, the famous Janey Canuck, was welcomed by the wealthy and powerful of Edmonton. She also, however, rode across the prairies and stopped to talk and visit women living on lonely homesteads. She heard many stories about the unfair laws of the times.

Because of laws brought over from Great Britain, the wives and children of Canada seemed to be owned by the husband and father. Emily was shocked to discover that a married woman could not own land, could not keep the money she earned herself and was not allowed the care and control of her children. Emily also learned that a man could sell the family farm, pocket the money and leave his wife and children behind to live in poverty. As well, if a man died without writing a will, his wife could not inherit anything from him, even the money she had earned herself or the land she had owned before her marriage.

The new province of Alberta had no laws to protect children or to protect the property of married women.

Emily set about to change the provincial laws. Emily had a wonderful memory and quickly became familiar with the laws. She worked to force the politicians to bring in new laws by giving speeches and, whenever possible, talking to elected members of Parliament. Newspapers eventually took up Emily's cause and her hard work paid off. In 1911, the Dower Act was passed in Alberta. This new law gave a woman a legal right to one third of her husband's estate during his life and after his death. A married woman in Alberta would not, however, be able to own

**A homestead in Canada's mid-west**

property in her own name until 1922.

Emily also researched and fought tirelessly for the Children's Protection Act that was passed to shelter children from their parents' abuse or neglect.

## NOTHING EVER HAPPENS BY CHANCE

The mid-west was a land of excitement and adventure. However, as more and more people arrived, the attitude of the time became "every man for himself!" Some families did well and became extremely wealthy. Some families, due to poor health or poor luck or poor skills, became destitute and many women and children suffered greatly as a result.

Emily emerged as a leader in the fight for social reform and for improved women's rights. Some people, comfortable with their own lives, called Emily a troublemaker. Emily, however, refused to stop fighting injustice. One of her favourite sayings was "nothing ever happens by chance; everything is pushed from behind." Emily knew that women working together could push from behind to improve all of society.

Emily encouraged other wealthy and prominent women to work for the benefit of all women. A master of organization, Emily coordinated groups of women to work together for common goals. She looked closely at prisons, hospitals and mental institutions and spoke up whenever she discovered dishonesty or poor management.

## VOTES FOR WOMEN

Emily believed women should have the vote and began to work closely with Nellie McClung, the suffragist from Manitoba, in the votes for women movement. If New Zealand had given all women the vote in 1893, why should Canada be so far behind? She became friends with Emmeline Pankhurst, the beautiful and famous leader of the votes for women movement in Great Britain, and traveled with Emmeline on speaking tours.

## HEAR NO EVIL, SEE NO EVIL

In the early 1900s a "good woman" was told to turn away from evil for just knowing about evil might somehow make her evil too. As a result most women did not know how the law treated the "other women"—the prostitutes who sold sexual favours for money. Often, however, these lawbreakers were lonely, young girls who fled to the city in search of work. Hungry, homeless, friendless, many young women were forced into prostitution or theft in order to stay alive.

The few "respectable" women who were concerned about the fate of these friendless other women were not able to make sure the women were treated fairly in court. The judges and lawyers, all men, refused to allow respectable women into the courtroom to watch the trials. The men claimed it was not proper for women and men to hear the evidence at the same time.

When Emily became aware of the problem, she suggested to the attorney-general of Alberta, that a special court be set up where only women would be present. The attorney-general remembered Emily's valiant fight to bring in the Dower Act and her knowledge of law. He quickly agreed to set up a women's court and, much to Emily's surprise, asked Emily to be the judge.

## JUDGE MURPHY

In 1916, Emily became the first woman magistrate in the British Empire. She encouraged her wealthy women friends to sit in her court and hear the sad, shocking stories of rape, assault, prostitution, child abuse and murder. Emily felt it was the duty of every woman to know what went on in the back streets of her city. "No woman," Emily wrote, "can become or remain degraded without all women suffering."

Armed with knowledge, Emily and her friends worked to set up homes for unwed mothers and schools that would teach a trade to young lawbreakers.

Alarmed at the number of pitiful drug addicts in her court, Emily wrote a book, *The Black Candle*, on the heroin, cocaine, opium and marijuana drug trade and on the frightening effects of drug addiction.

## A JUDGE BUT NOT A PERSON

Emily also had her own battles for acceptance in a world controlled by men. The idea of a woman judge threatened some men who did their best to make Emily's job difficult. Her first day in court one of the criminal lawyers objected to Emily being the judge in the case. He argued that only a "qualified person" could be a judge and, in the eyes of the law, a woman was not a "person." Emily recorded his objection and then calmly continued with the case. Other lawyers also picked up the argument and constantly challenged Emily's right to be a judge.

In 1920 the question of whether a woman was a person in law came before Alberta's Supreme Court. The court decided that, according to the laws of Alberta, a woman was a person. Emily's position as a woman judge in Alberta was now safe, but what about the legal rights of women outside Alberta? Emily wanted all Canadian women to be able to hold important positions.

## A FEEBLE EXCUSE

At one time in Canada, the British North America Act of 1867 set out the powers and responsibilities of the provinces and of the federal government. This federal act used the word *persons* when it referred to more than one person and the word *he* when it referred to one person. Therefore, many argued, the act was really saying that only a man could be a person. If only a man could be a person, then when the act also said only "qualified persons" could be appointed to the Canadian Senate, then only men could be appointed to the Senate. The earlier decision of the Alberta Supreme Court, a provincial court, that women were persons had no power over the federal laws of Canada.

Women's groups began pressuring the federal government to appoint a woman to the Senate. Many wanted the highly respected, hard-working Emily Murphy to have the honour of being the first woman Senator. Three Prime Ministers in a row, however, refused to appoint a woman Senator. They used the same, lame argument that women could not be appointed because women were not persons in federal law. It was obvious, however, that the persons argument was a feeble excuse to keep women out of important positions.

## THE PERSONS CASE

After ten years of delay on the part of the federal government, Emily decided it was time for action. As her friend, Nellie McClung put it, "Mrs. Murphy loved a fight and so far as I know, never turned her back on one."

So in 1927 Emily and four other prominent Canadian women— Nellie Mooney McClung, Irene Marryat Parlby, Louis Crummy McKinney and Henrietta Muir Edwards—asked the Supreme Court of Canada to answer the question "Are women persons?" After five weeks of debate and argument the Supreme Court of Canada decided that the word *person* did not include women.

The five women, nicknamed "The Valiant Five" were shocked by the Supreme Court decision but did not give up the fight. Instead, they refused to accept the decision and took the Persons Case to the Privy Council in England which, in those days, was Canada's highest court. The women of Canada rejoiced when the Privy Council finally announced, on 18 October 1929, that Canadian women were indeed persons.

## A JUDGE BUT NOT A SENATOR

Emily's hard work and perseverance—she wrote more than seven hundred letters to powerful people during the Persons Case—opened many doors for Canadian women. The federal government could no longer delay appointing a woman to the Senate in Ottawa.

Thousands of Canadians believed Emily Murphy was the logical choice for the Senate, but it was not to be. Although each member of the Valiant Five was qualified for such a position, not one was ever offered a Senate appointment—an act of spite, perhaps, on the part of the federal government.

## A FIGHTER TO THE END

Emily Ferguson Murphy died quietly in her sleep at the age of sixty-five. She had retired as a judge two years earlier, but continued researching, writing and fighting injustice up to the day of her death.

Later, when asked why the widely known and well-respected Emily Murphy had never been honoured with an appointment to the quiet, dignified Senate, a government official shrugged and replied, "She'd have made too much trouble, of course!"

Further Suggested Reading:

James, Donna. *Emily Murphy*. Toronto: Fitzhenry & Whiteside Limited, 1977.

Mander, Christine. *Emily Murphy: Rebel*. Toronto: Simon & Pierre, 1985.

# CHAPTER 14

## ARTIST   AUTHOR   REBEL

# EMILY CARR
## —— (1871 - 1945) ——

**I could not paint in the old way—it is dead—meaningless—empty.**
**—Emily Carr**

*Drenched to the skin, Emily crouched inside the ruined grave house, listening to the rain pounding on the roof. The dank smell of rotting wood filled the gloom and mosquitoes hummed and buzzed in a frenzy about her head.*

*Emily's thoughts turned to Kitwancool—the forbidden village. It was a dangerous place—even the Mounted Police would only visit in a group. Emily Carr, however, was not frightened by the stories. She swatted a mosquito and came to a decision. Her next stop would be Kitwancool.*

## THE POWER OF NATURE

Emily Carr was born in Victoria, British Columbia, in 1871. Her English parents expected their children to behave like proper English ladies and gentlemen. Emily's four older sisters did what they were told and always acted like ladies. Strong-willed Emily did not.

Both parents died when Emily was in her teens and her older sister Edith ran the household with an iron hand. Emily rebelled and was often whipped for standing up to Edith on behalf of herself and her younger brother. As an escape, Emily would ride her pony out into the silent forests. There, she first discovered nature's glory and power.

## THE ONLY PLACE TO LEARN

Emily had always loved to draw. For three years she studied art at the California School of Design in San Francisco. In 1893 her family told her she had "played at art" long enough, and she returned to Victoria.

She turned the loft of the family cow barn into an art studio and began giving drawing and painting lessons to children. Emily was full of life and full of fun. The children enjoyed their lessons and she soon had many students.

European artists who visited the west coast, however, told Emily the

**Rebellious young Emily with her sisters. Emily is in the lower right corner.**

***Three Indian Girls, Ucluelet*** **by Emily Carr, 1898. In the early years, Emily used a realistic style of sketching and painting.**

only place to learn to paint was in Paris, France, or in London, England. Emily immediately began to save her money so that she could study art in England.

## UCLUELET

Emily's sisters were very religious and the Carr house was often full of missionaries who wanted to convert the West Coast First Nations to Christianity. One missionary invited Emily to spend the summer sketching the area around Ucluelet and the West Coast Mission.

Emily eagerly accepted the offer and spent the summer of 1898 sketching the people, houses, totem poles and canoes of the native village. She did not know the native language and had to act out what she was trying to say, often breaking into laughter at her own efforts. The people of Ucluelet liked her and called her Klee Wyck or Laughing One.

Emily admired the native people and their way of life. They did not fight or try to tame nature but lived in harmony with what was around them. She felt the missionaries were wrong to talk the native people into changing their religion and way of life.

Visiting European artists had grandly told Emily that Canada's west coast scenery could not be painted and so she did not try. Years later Emily realized those artists had been frightened by Canada's vast size and wild spaces. Unable to capture Canada's "bigness" on canvas, the

European artists had blamed the land rather than their own lack of talent.

Emily, however, moved by the fierce beauty around her, longed to paint the rain forests and rugged shorelines of the west coast. She hoped that study abroad would help her find the way to paint the country she loved.

## MERRY OLD ENGLAND

By 1899, Emily had saved enough money to study art in England. Her parents and all their English friends had always talked longingly of London, but when Emily arrived she hated the city. It was dusty, crowded, noisy and smelly. The parks were tidy and tame with prim signs that read Please Do Not Walk On The Grass or Please Do Not Whistle, Sing Or Shout.

Emily spent five years in England. She was proud to be Canadian and did not try to become English. She studied very hard at the Westminster School of Art in London, always pushing herself to take more and more art classes and learn as much as possible before her money ran out.

Emily was very attractive with lovely gray eyes, dark eyebrows and curly brown hair. One of her many admirers came all the way from Victoria to propose marriage. Emily hated England and longed for Canada, but she refused to return to Victoria with the young man and become his wife. She wanted to continue her studies. For Emily, art was more than just something people did in their spare time.

Emily drove herself at her work until she collapsed and was ill for over a year. When she sailed for home, Emily felt the five years she had spent in England had been a waste of time.

## THE POWER OF NATIVE ART

In 1905, Emily opened a studio in the rapidly growing city of Vancouver and began giving art lessons to children. Emily saw, with alarm, that the totem poles and the native way of life she admired were both crumbling away. Emily decided to record the art of the totem pole before it vanished. She spent her summers painting totem poles and native villages. With only her sketch sack, food supplies and her dog Ginger Pop, Emily traveled long distances to native villages such as Skedans, Tanoo, and Cumshewa. She trudged along narrow, bumpy roads, or begged rides with fishing boats or with native families traveling up the coast in tiny gas-powered boats.

By living with the people and becoming their friend, Emily began to understand their art. The totem poles told tales of ancestors and of

**Emily Carr's *Big Raven*, painted in 1928, appeared on a Canadian postage stamp. Emily used her early sketches to paint later works of art.**

strange land and sea creatures. The wooden carvings showed how each artist felt about the thing being carved. They were not trying to show how the bird or animal looked in nature, but to show its fierceness or its grace or its cunning. Shapes were sometimes twisted or altered on totem poles to show these deeper meanings.

Understanding native art gave Emily a new way of looking at the world around her. She wanted to capture on paper the powerful feelings the totem artists had carved into the wood, but she did not know how.

## A NEW WAY IN FRANCE

Emily began to hear about artists in France who were using colour, light and shape in their paintings in a new way. These artists did not want to show only the surface of a subject. Like the totem artists, they wanted to show how they felt when they were painting the scene. Some people liked the New Art; most hated it.

Emily again saved up enough money to study abroad. In the summer of 1910 she traveled with Alice, her favourite sister, to Paris, France, to learn about this new way of seeing.

Emily visited artists' studios and was both shocked and attracted by the New Art. She took art lessons in Paris but soon became ill and spent three months in hospital. Through history, great artists such as Van Gogh, Cezanne and Gaugin found that big cities made them ill. Emily was no exception. The French doctor told Emily if she did not keep out of big cities she would die.

Emily recovered her health and continued her studies in the French countryside. There she sketched and painted in the new way of seeing. At a time when great artists such as Monet, Renoir and Degas were working in Paris, two of Emily's paintings were shown in the important Paris rebel art exhibition Salon D'Automne of 1911. Emily then returned to British Columbia and brought the New Art back to Vancouver.

## REBEL WITH A CAUSE

When Emily exhibited her paintings from France created in the new way, they were openly laughed at and scorned. People still expected to see paintings with the type of detail they could see in a photograph. Vancouver people hated the clear colours, simple shapes and sweeping brush strokes of New Art. Parents would no longer send their children to Emily's classes. Vancouver art schools where Emily had once taught, now refused to hire her.

Emily used the village sketches she had made years earlier and painted large canvases in the new way. When she held a show of her new work it was laughed at and insulted. Her sisters felt disgraced by her new kind of art and begged her to go back to her old style. For Emily, however, the old style of painting was dead. She refused to give up the new way of seeing; she believed it held the key to capturing on canvas the wild, brooding beauty of the West Coast. The West Coast natives liked her art, but no one else did.

In the summer of 1912 she traveled with her sheepdog Billie to sketch and paint remote native villages in the Queen Charlotte Islands and Skeena River area. However, with no pupils and no one buying her pictures, lack of money forced Emily to return to Victoria in 1913.

## DARK DAYS

Since no one would buy her art, Emily was forced to make her living in other ways. She built and ran a boarding house in Victoria, doing all the cooking, cleaning and building repairs herself. She raised and sold hundreds of Old English sheepdogs. Using native designs, Emily began to weave rugs and make pottery which tourists eagerly bought. Her pots would sell; her paintings would not.

For fifteen years Emily struggled to pay her bills—too busy to create paintings that nobody would buy. Most of her canvases were stored away. Emily's boarders made insulting comments about the few paintings which she hung on her boardinghouse walls. Yet in spite of her disappointments, Emily was still lively and witty and fun. Emily seemed younger, said a friend, than people half her age. She told wonderful stories about her many trips and adventures. The love and friendship of Alice and Lizzie, two of her older sisters, also helped her through these dark years. As an artist, however, Emily felt alone and "on the edge of nowhere."

## STILL A REBEL

A rebel even in her fifties, Emily constantly shocked prim Victoria. She hated snobs and refused to be polite to people she did not like. She also bluntly said what she thought, regardless of whom she upset.

Emily never outgrew her love of animals and always surrounded herself with pets—dogs, a white rat, bullfinches, parrots, a cockatoo and even a monkey named Woo. When she went shopping, she pushed her monkey Woo to the stores in a baby carriage. On the way home, Emily filled the baby carriage with supplies while Woo happily scampered beside her.

## GROUP OF SEVEN

Emily was amazed when, in 1927, she was invited to exhibit some of her canvases in an exhibition of Canadian West Coast Art. The director of the National Art Gallery in Ottawa had heard about her paintings through the West Coast First Nations people.

She learned about a new Canadian art movement called the Group of Seven and visited some of the members of the group on her way to see her own exhibition in Ottawa. She understood their art immediately. Emily became friends with Lawren Harris, the leader of the Group of Seven. Harris praised Emily's work and later wrote letters of support and advice.

## NO LONGER ON THE EDGE OF NOWHERE

Emily, inspired by the art of the Group of Seven and encouraged by the success of the exhibition of Canadian West Coast Art, returned to Victoria and began painting again at a feverish pace.

At age 57, Emily made her last trip north to remote native villages. She braved huge swarms of mosquitoes and wild Pacific storms. Alone, she visited the forbidden village of Kitwancool. Armed only with her art supplies, Emily became friends with the people of Kitwancool and painted their totem poles.

After 1928 Emily decided to try to paint the west coast scenery that had frightened so many artists. Instead of native subjects, she began to paint the movement and sweeping power she felt in the forests, fields and skies around her. Emily often sketched and painted outdoors with Woo and her dogs.

She became an honorary member of the Group of Seven and her paintings were shown in Canada, Europe and the United States. She made new friends and her studio became a friendly gathering place for

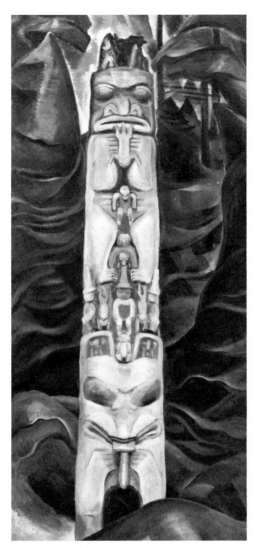

***Totem and Forest* by Emily Carr, 1931. Emily admired the way totem artists carved powerful feelings into the wood.**

visiting writers, musicians and artists. Emily no longer felt that she lived on the edge of nowhere.

Her art, however, still puzzled many people and few of her paintings were sold. Some she sold to friends for fifteen or twenty dollars when she was desperate for money.

## EMILY CARR, AUTHOR

Emily finally got rid of her boardinghouse and spent much of her time painting. At age sixty-six she had a heart attack and could no longer paint alone in the forests. Emily, however, could not remain idle. She wrote short stories about her adventures in the native villages she had visited years earlier.

Emily wrote the way she painted—by cutting out as much as possible. She called her book *Klee Wyck*—the name the native people had given her as a young woman. Emily's book was published when she was seventy. *Klee Wyck* was a tremendous success and won the Governor General's medal for literature. She wrote a total of seven books including *The Book of Small*, *The House of All Sorts*, and *Growing Pains*.

Victoria did not understand Emily Carr the painter, but they loved Emily Carr the author. Emily enjoyed the attention her home town now showered upon her.

*Above the Gravel Pit* by Emily Carr, painted around 1936 or 1937. This is an example of the sweeping lines and huge skies Emily used in her later years to capture the bigness of Canada's West Coast.

In 1944 Emily's paintings were exhibited in Montreal and out of the sixty paintings exhibited, fifty-seven were sold. The public finally understood Emily's new way of seeing.

She died peacefully the next year at age seventy-three, painting and writing up to the very end.

## GENEROUS GIFT

Emily Carr, gifted with both the pen and the brush, waited many years for public recognition. Her first major art exhibition took place when she was fifty-six; her first book was published when she was seventy. Yet before Emily died, she had the pleasure of knowing her lively books were selling well and her paintings admired as great art.

In a generous gesture, Emily left many of her best works to the Province of British Columbia. Today the Vancouver Art Gallery proudly displays the paintings of Emily Carr—artist, author and rebel.

Further Suggested Reading:

Neering, Rosemary. *Emily Carr*. Toronto: Fitzhenry & Whiteside Limited, 1975.

Norcross, E. Blanche. *Pioneers Every One*, Burns and MacEachern, 1979.

# CHAPTER 15

## AUTHOR

# LUCY MAUD MONTGOMERY

## —— (1874 - 1942) ——

**I enjoy my success for I've worked and thought hard for it. I have the satisfaction, too, of knowing that I've fought my own battles.**
**—Lucy Maud Montgomery**

*Maud shivered as she rummaged through the chilly clothes room. She was small and slim and the cold Prince Edward Island winter chilled her to the bone. She peeked inside a hat box, then smiled sadly as she lifted out a thick, typewritten manuscript. Her first novel! After being turned down by four publishing companies, Maud had put the manuscript away and forgotten all about it.*

*Maud began flipping through the manuscript, stopping to read the occasional page. She felt a growing excitement. This really was a good piece of work! She decided it deserved one last chance.*

*Maud mailed her novel to a fifth publishing company. This time the manuscript was accepted for publication and Anne of Green Gables, set in Maud's beloved Prince Edward Island, became an immediate, worldwide success. Maud Montgomery— and Prince Edward Island—would never be the same.*

## A MOTHERLESS CHILD

Lucy Maud Montgomery was born in Clifton, Prince Edward Island, on 30 November 1874—the year after her province joined Canada. She was always called Maud.

Maud was not yet two when her mother died of tuberculosis. Maud's father sent her to live with her grandparents, Lucy and Alexander Macneill. Her grandparents lived on a farm on the north side of Prince Edward Island, near the tiny settlement of Cavendish. Maud loved Cavendish and often used it as the setting for her short stories and books.

As a child, Maud saw herself as an orphan because her father had poetry. Her strict Presbyterian grandparents felt Maud should turn her mind away from such unimportant things on that holy day. On Sundays, therefore, Maud could only read books of sermons or a book about Christian missionaries.

It was Maud's rich, imaginary life, however, that probably gave her the greatest pleasure as a child. When six-year-old Maud saw her own, dim reflection in the glass doors of the bookcase, she pretended they were friends who had names and different personalities. She made up poetic names for her favourite places around Cavendish—Lover's Lane, Lake of Shining Waters, Dryad's Bubble. Young Maud even created and wrote down the life stories of her dolls and cats. She also kept a journal from the time she was nine.

## A VISIT TO FATHER

Maud's father settled in the booming town of Prince Albert, Saskatchewan, remarried and started a new family. Maud, who loved her father dearly, was delighted to travel out west and live with her father and her new stepmother. Sixteen-year-old Maud made the trip with her grand-

**The gate into Lover's Lane. Maud loved Lover's Lane and wrote that she was happier there than anywhere else.**

**Maud loved cats and enjoyed taking photographs. Pictured above is her photograph of the kitchen at Cavendish where she started her novel *Anne of Green Gables*.**

moved out west to seek his fortune when Maud was young. Maud, with her warm, fun-loving nature, found it hard to live with aging grandparents who were stern and strict and set in their ways. As well, Maud's many relatives felt free to scold and criticize a motherless child.

All her life Maud remembered and bitterly resented this part of her childhood. Years later, her stories would often be about orphaned or motherless children.

## A LIVELY IMAGINATION

Much of Maud's childhood, however, was wonderful. Outgoing and full of life, she had many friends and enjoyed school in the nearby, one-room schoolhouse. Maud had an excellent memory and, without much effort on her part, was often top of her class.

Her grandparents' house was full of books, and Maud read whenever possible. On Sundays, however, she was not allowed to read novels or

Maud at age twenty-four, eight years before she wrote *Anne of Green Gables*.

father, Senator Donald Montgomery. Maud loved her Grandfather Montgomery, who treated her with kindness and gentleness.

Her trip in August of 1890, started with a train ride she would never forget. Her grandfather, who was a friend of Canada's first Prime Minister, Sir John A. Macdonald, arranged for them to have a short train ride with Sir John and Lady Macdonald who were on a tour of Prince Edward Island. Maud rode on the Prime Minister's special train and was thrilled to sit between Sir John and Lady Macdonald.

In Saskatchewan, Maud's reunion with her father was a joyful one. Unfortunately she soon developed a strong dislike for her young stepmother who Maud thought was jealous, sulky and mean.

Maud loved Prince Albert, which was nestled in a river valley and surrounded by forests and lakes, but often felt homesick for her beloved Cavendish. Her life in Prince Albert, however, was a busy one and she attended high school where she was a popular student.

Her high school teacher fell in love with Maud and often dropped in for evening visits. Sixteen-year-old Maud disliked the man and had no trouble in saying no when he eventually proposed.

While in Prince Albert, Maud continued writing her stories and poems and was thrilled when a Charlottetown newspaper printed one of her poems on its front page. However, she missed more and more time away from school in order to look after her baby half brother and do housework for her stepmother. Maud grew more and more unhappy with her stepmother until, in 1891, she said good-bye to her beloved father and returned to live with her grandparents in Prince Edward Island.

## A TEACHING CAREER

At twenty-one Maud became a school teacher, one of the few respectable careers open to a woman in those days. Maud's real goal, however, was to become a writer. Even as a busy teacher, she would get up at 6:00 a.m. every day and write for an hour. In the winter, her room was often so cold that, as she wrote, she would have to put on her winter coat and sit on her feet to keep them from freezing.

She spent her first year of teaching in Bideford, Prince Edward Island. She also spent a year at Dalhousie University in Nova Scotia.

Maud then taught in Belmont, Prince Edward Island.  Maud had enjoyed herself at university, but she was bitterly unhappy in Belmont. She disliked the family she had to live with, and spent much of the winter shivering with cold in the drafty house. One morning she even woke up to find her pillow covered with snow!

In Belmont, Maud also received the sad news that her best friend from Prince Albert, Saskatchewan, Willie Pritchard, had died from the 'flu. Although Maud had never been in love with Willie, he had been a close friend and they had often written to each other. Years later she would still read his old letters and feel the loss.

Maud left her teaching job at Belmont with relief and went on to teach school at Bedeque. In Bedeque she fell deeply in love with a young farmer. The two had nothing in common, however, and Maud knew she would never marry her secret love. While in Bedeque, Maud's Grandfather Macneill died, and Maud moved back to Cavendish to look after her Grandmother Macneill and the old farmhouse.

One year later Maud was shocked to hear that the young man she had so deeply loved while in Bedeque had, like Willie Pritchard, caught the 'flu and died. Six months later, Maud's father, whom she still adored, suddenly died of pneumonia. Stunned by so many deaths, Maud found that writing helped her to forget her sorrow. As well, she was now beginning to earn small amounts of money from her many poems and short stories.

## A NEWSPAPER WOMAN

In 1901 Maud arranged for a relative to move in with her Grandmother Macneill in Cavendish while she herself started a new career in Charlottetown. Maud worked as a proofreader and columnist for a newspaper called the *Daily Echo*. As proofreader, her job was to catch and correct any mistakes in grammar or spelling before the newspaper was printed.

Once a week Maud wrote an article for the paper called Around the Tea Table, which she wrote under the name of Cynthia. In it she chatted about "fun, fashions, fads, fancies."

Maud, although homesick for Cavendish, enjoyed her work at the *Daily Echo*, and the people she met. Her pay, however, was five dollars a week for a six-day work week, and she needed to make more money to live in the city. Unfortunately Maud was now too tired to write in the early mornings or at night. Her solution was to spend every spare moment at the office writing her stories and poems.

Maud discovered she did not have to be alone in a quiet room to use her imagination. Instead, she learned to write surrounded by the noise and confusion of machinery and ringing telephones. Soon she was again earning that extra money she needed so badly. One magazine even paid Maud twenty-five dollars for one of her stories.

**Red-haired, green-eyed Willie Pritchard, was Maud's close friend when she lived in Prince Albert, Saskatchewan. Willie died in his early twenties.**

## SECRET ENGAGEMENT

Maud worked nine months at the *Daily Echo* then decided to return to Cavendish because her eighty-year-old grandmother needed her at home. Maud spent the next nine years living with and looking after her grandmother. During this time Maud had a quiet, but busy life. Her letters and her journals, however, show that she was secretly lonely and unhappy. She longed to marry and have children of her own, yet she was expected to live and care for Grandmother Macneill as long as the woman was alive. As well, her Grandmother Macneill had become even more sour and set in her ways and did not like lonely Maud to have visitors.

Again Maud's only escape from this unhappy time in her life was her writing. In addition to poems and stories, she wrote open and honest letters to two pen pals she had never met—a farmer in Alberta and a journalist in Scotland.

In 1906, at the age of thirty-two, Maud became secretly engaged to Reverend Ewan Macdonald, a man she respected but did not love. Ewan, a Presbyterian minister, agreed they would not marry until Grandmother Macneill was dead.

## ANNE OF GREEN GABLES

Maud spent the fall and winter of 1906 writing her first novel. In the past, Maud had found she could not sell stories unless they preached proper values at all times. However, for her first novel, Maud took a chance and did not include high, moral messages in *Anne of Green Gables*. Instead she wrote about a lonely, warm-hearted orphan who, in spite of her faults, finds a loving home in the beautiful countryside of Prince Edward Island.

When a publishing company in Boston, Massachusetts, finally agreed to publish *Anne of Green Gables*, Maud was given a choice. She could sell the book rights for a one time amount of five hundred dollars or receive a small sum of money, called a royalty, for each book sold. Fortunately, Maud chose to receive royalty payments for, to the surprise of both Maud and her publishing company, *Anne of Green Gables* was an immediate best-seller. When it was printed in June of 1908, demand for the book was so high that it had to be reprinted six times in the next five months. Maud's first royalty cheque was for $1,730 and she would receive many large royalty cheques in the years to come.

Meanwhile, readers were begging for more books about lovable, red-headed Anne Shirley. Maud would eventually write a total of eight Anne books.

# BITTERSWEET FAME

Maud's years of hard work had finally paid off—she was now a successful writer. Yet she found the fruits of fame were bittersweet. Some
friends and relatives were coldly jealous. Strangers were now curious
about Maud and tourists in Prince Edward Island demanded to meet the
famous L. M. Montgomery.

There were bright spots in her life, such as the time Governor
General Earl Grey made a special request to meet the author of *Anne of
Green Gables*. She was also pleased by the letter of praise she received
from Mark Twain, the famous American author of *Tom Sawyer* and
*Huckleberry Finn*.

For the most part, however, Maud continued her quiet, lonely,
unhappy life with Grandmother Macneill, longing for a home and family
of her own, while writing about the life and loves of an orphan named
Anne Shirley.

# PERFECT

After the death of Grandmother Macneill in 1911, Maud, age thirty-
seven, married Reverend Ewan Macdonald and found herself with
another difficult career. Maud was now "the minister's wife" and as such
was expected to be a woman without flaws or faults. In those days
everything the minister's wife did and said was closely watched by the
entire community. Maud took her new role very much to heart and never
again felt she could just be herself.

Maud left behind her beloved Prince Edward Island and moved with
Ewan to Leaskdale, Ontario, and then, fifteen years later, to Norval,
Ontario.

In addition to carrying out the many duties expected of the minister's
wife, Maud raised their two sons and continued her successful writing
career, writing a total of twenty-two books—twenty of them for children.
She wrote in her journal that she received fan mail from people all over
the world: "men and women who are grandparents, boys at school and
college, old pioneers in the Australian bush, missionaries in China,
monks in remote monasteries, and red-headed girls all over the world."

In 1923 Maud was the first Canadian woman to become a Fellow of
the Royal Society of Arts in England and in 1935 she was invested with
the Order of the British Empire.

Her married life, although busy, was not happy.  The exhausting list
of joyless duties expected of her took up most of Maud's time and
energy. Her third son was stillborn. In 1919 Maud was further devastated

**Maud married Reverend Ewan Macdonald and took on the exhausting and difficult job of minister's wife. Maud wrote in her journal, "Those whom the gods wish to destroy they make ministers' wives."**

when her dearest friend, her cousin Frederica Campbell, died of pneumonia at the age of thirty-six. As well, her husband Ewan became tormented by long periods of low spirits and black despair. With her trusted Frederica dead, Maud had no one with whom she could share her troubles and her sorrows. Maud was afraid her husband's growing mental illness would cause him to lose his job. Feeling alone and friendless, she struggled to keep Ewan's behaviour and mood swings a secret. The stress and strain of constantly putting on a cheerful face for the world, often made Maud herself ill with worry and secret despair.

When Ewan retired in 1935, the family moved to Toronto where Maud spent the rest of her life writing. Maud died in 1942 at the age of sixty-eight and was buried in the cemetery of her beloved Cavendish.

## ANNE LIVES ON

As the setting for many of Maud's books, Prince Edward Island became a popular tourist attraction. While Maud was still alive, the Canadian government responded by setting up a national park. Centred around Cavendish, the park still preserves the lovely places Maud described in her books—Lover's Lane, Dryad's Bubble, Lake of Shining Waters.

Maud Montgomery's books are as popular today, as they were when they were first written. The books have been translated into thirty languages and millions of copies have been sold worldwide. Maud's books have also been made into movies, musicals and a popular television series.

Whether the reader is a young Canadian girl or a British Prime Minister, Maud's books have charmed millions. Today, Lucy Maud Montgomery is still one of Canada's most widely read authors.

Further Suggested Reading:

Gillen, Mollie. *Lucy Maud Montgomery*. Toronto: Fitzhenry & Whiteside, 1978.

Rubio, Mary and Elizabeth Waterston, eds. *The Selected Journals of L. M. Montgomery*. 3 vols. Toronto: Oxford University Press, 1985.

# CHAPTER 16

## SUFFRAGIST

# NELLIE MOONEY MCCLUNG

## —— (1873 - 1951) ——

**Never retract, never explain, never apologize; get the thing done and let them howl.**

**—Nellie Mooney McClung**

*Attractive, dark-haired Nellie McClung faced the crowded room and began her talk. She was a powerful speaker and the crowd hung on Nellie's every word. As she spoke, they laughed at her quick wit; they also sadly shook their heads at her stories of wasted, despairing lives. Women must be given the vote, she told them.*

*However, not everyone in the audience agreed. In the middle of her talk, one man shouted out, "Aw, don't you wish you were a man right now, Nellie?"*

*Nellie smiled sweetly. "Don't you wish **you** were?" she shot back.*

*The crowd roared with laughter and the heckler fell into red-faced silence. No one could get the better of Nellie McClung.*

## CHOOSING A MOTHER-IN-LAW

Nellie, the sixth child of John and Letitia Mooney, was born in 1873. She grew up on her family's farm in Manitoba and then became a teacher at age fifteen.

When Nellie graduated from teacher's college her first job was in the tiny hamlet of Somerset, Manitoba. When Nellie got off the train in Somerset, she was told the crops had been flattened by hail, so the hamlet had no money for salaries. Nellie received her room and board with a local family, but no teacher's pay!

That first year, Nellie was impressed with Mrs J. A. McClung, wife of the Methodist minister for the nearby town of Manitou. After their first meeting, Nellie said of Mrs McClung, "She is the only woman I have ever seen whom I should like to have for a mother-in-law." A few

**151**

**Nellie McClung wrote, "I have never desired the approval or even tolerance of the people whose interests run contrary to the public good, the people who believe if they are happy and prosperous, all's well with the world."**

years later the same Mrs McClung did indeed become Nellie's mother-in-law when Nellie married handsome, young Wesley McClung. Nellie never regretted her marriage and fifty years later cheerfully claimed, "The day I married Wes, I did the best day's work I have ever done."

## NO VOTE—NO RIGHTS

The next years were busy ones for Nellie. She and Wesley had five children and Nellie, encouraged by her mother-in-law, began a writing career. Nellie was thrilled when the famous Canadian poet, Pauline Johnson, put on two concerts in the little town of Manitou. Pauline was a dinner guest of the McClung's and Nellie was charmed by her grace and beauty.

Nellie's own home life was full and happy. Her husband Wes, was a wonderful man, and she dearly loved her children. Nellie, however, was disturbed by the hardship and despair she saw in other people's lives.

# STILL TOO DELICATE TO VOTE

Champion Lady Steer Roper of the World, Winnipeg Stampede, 1913.

Doukhobor women threshing grain

# STILL TOO DELICATE TO VOTE

**Canadian Service Women, World War I**

Canada was a very different place in the 1800s, because a woman was not a person in the eyes of the law. As soon as a woman married, everything she owned—even her jewelry and clothing—by law belonged to her husband. As well, once she was married, any wages she earned or anything she inherited belonged to her husband.

The husband also owned their children and he alone decided whether they should go to school, what their religion should be, and at what age the children would be sent out to work (as early as age six in some cases). When the father died, he could leave the children in his will to someone else, even if their mother was alive and able to look after the children.

As well, the husband could beat his wife and children whenever he felt like it for there was no law to stop him.

## ALCOHOL

Communities were also plagued by alcohol abuse. In those days, women were discouraged from drinking any alcohol. Men, however, usually drank to get drunk. The idea of drinking in moderation only one or two glasses of alcohol at one time was not part of that period. It was not uncommon for men to drink away their wages or their farm profits in a tavern in town, and then come home and beat their wives and children in

Women solder fuses in a Quebec munitions factory during World War I. Women did not get the vote in the Province of Quebec until 1940.

a drunken rage. The wives and children in such cases had no one to turn to for help, because what was happening to them was not against the law.

Women did not have the right to vote, so they could not pressure their members of Parliament to pass laws that would treat women and children fairly.

## TEMPERANCE

Women decided to take action against the hardship and violence caused by widespread drunkenness. A group called the Women's Christian Temperance Union was formed to work for prohibition (stopping the sale of all beer, wine and liquor). Nellie's first book, *Sowing Seeds in Danny*, had been a success, and Nellie's mother-in-law arranged for Nellie to read from her popular book at local Temperance Union meetings. From merely reading aloud from her book, Nellie soon began to speak at the meetings. She, too, believed that prohibition was the only way to put an end to the widespread drunkenness that was destroying so many lives. It became obvious that Nellie was a gifted public speaker whose talents the Temperance Union could put to good use.

## A BETTER PLACE TO LIVE

Women were tired of being told they were too delicate to vote and they often discussed politics at the Temperance Union meetings. Some women agreed with Nellie that the prohibition laws would not be passed until women were granted the vote. Once women had the vote, Nellie felt that women would vote for politicians who promised to bring in prohibition. Nellie also felt that with the vote, women would push for other laws that would make Canada a better place to live.

The word *suffrage* means the right to vote, and women who worked for the right of women to vote, were called Suffragists or Suffragettes. Some members of the Temperance Union became suffragists and Nellie McClung was one of them. Not all suffragists, however, were members of the Temperance Union or believed in prohibition.

Nellie began spending a great deal of time writing and speaking out in favour of women's suffrage and prohibition. She spoke at over four hundred public meetings in twenty years, often speaking three times a day. Nellie's speaking tours took her across Canada, as well as to the United States and Great Britain. She soon became famous, but not all the attention she received was friendly.

## UNDER ATTACK

At the time Nellie began her long career of public speaking, any woman who did not devote every minute of her life to looking after her family was often criticized for neglecting her family. Nellie, who wrote sixteen books in her life, made enough money from her work to hire household help. Her wonderful mother-in-law was also a great support. However, like many suffragists, Nellie was criticized for neglecting her family. The McClungs turned these false accusations aside with good humour. As a joke, Wes McClung taught their youngest son, three-year-old Mark, to entertain visiting suffragists and other guests by lisping sadly, "I am the son of a suffragette, and have never known a mother's love."

As well, the beer and liquor companies and others who did not want women to have the vote tried to portray suffragists and Temperance Union members as bitter, ugly, man-hating women. It was difficult, however, to make such accusations about Nellie McClung who was deeply involved in both the temperance and suffrage movements. Attractive, happily married, the mother of five children—four of whom were sons—it was impossible to argue that Nellie McClung was a woman who hated men.

Most of all, however, Nellie was a wonderful speaker, and people flocked to hear her speak. Once, when she spoke in Toronto's Massey Hall, the hall was packed until there was standing room only. Thousands more were turned away at the door, unable to squeeze into the building.

## THE WOMEN'S PARLIAMENT

Nellie McClung belonged to the Canadian Women's Press Club as well as the Political Equality League that was formed in 1912 to work for female suffrage. The women worked for the right to vote by giving speeches, attending conferences and trying to talk elected politicians into supporting their cause.

The work was slow and hard and in Manitoba, one of the women's greatest obstacles was the Premier of Manitoba, Sir Rodmond Roblin. In an interview with Nellie, Premier Roblin laughingly refused all requests for female suffrage. "I don't want a hyena in petticoats talking politics at me," he scolded Nellie, "I want a nice, gentle creature to bring me my slippers." Roblin, however, soon discovered the power of the women's movement in the province of Manitoba.

On 27 January 1914, a delegation representing groups such as the Political Equality League, the Women's Christian Temperance Union, the Canadian Women's Press Club and the YWCA appeared before the

Manitoba Parliament and asked that women be given the vote in Manitoba's provincial elections.

Nellie led the delegation and, as she expected, the women's request was turned down. However, she listened and watched carefully as Premier Roblin, scornful as always of the women having the vote, gave a pompous speech and refused their request. Nellie paid careful attention to Premier Roblin's speech. She was a wonderful mimic and would soon be using one of the most powerful weapons of all—humour.

The next evening, in a packed Winnipeg theatre, the women of the Politician Equality League put on play called The Women's Parliament. In the play, men had pitifully few legal rights and could not vote, but all the members of Parliament were women. Just as in a real parliament, the women members of Parliament asked questions, made motions and read bills. The women had a wonderful time mocking the Manitoba Parliament.

At one point a delegation of men arrived with a petition that men be given the right to vote. "We have brains," the men pleaded, "why not let us vote?"

Nellie, playing the lead role of premier, mimicked Premier Roblin's voice and gestures perfectly. The audience in the theatre laughed with recognition as she gave a scornful reply to the men's request; a reply that turned upside down all of the arguments that had been used against the women in the real Parliament, only the day before.

As premier, Nellie grandly told the men, "The trouble is that if men start to vote, they will vote too much. Politics unsettles men, and unsettled men means unsettled bills, broken furniture, broken vows and—divorce . . . If men were to get into the habit of voting—who knows what might happen—it's hard enough to keep them home now. History is full of unhappy examples of men in public life—Nero, Herod, King John . . . ." Again and again the crowd roared with laughter.

The play was a tremendous success. The newspapers praised the event: "Sir Rodmond's Weak Position Assailed by Winnipeg Women and his Old-Fashioned Theories Exploded . . . " and "Women Score in Drama and Debate . . . " ran some of the headlines. More and more people were convinced that women should have the vote.

## A FIRST FOR MANITOBA

In May 1915, political scandals forced Premier Roblin to resign. Suffragists rejoiced because the new Premier, T. C. Norris, had always promised to support votes for women. Once in power, however, Premier

Norris changed his mind. He said he would not introduce a women's suffrage bill into Parliament unless the suffragists could show there was popular support for the bill. Again the suffragists rose to the challenge. They collected a petition supporting female suffrage containing over 40,000 signatures. One ninety-four-year-old woman had gathered 4,250 signatures all by herself!

Premier Norris could not ignore such a large petition and on 27 January 1916 the Bill for the Enfranchisement of Women was passed unanimously. Women in Manitoba now had the vote as well as the right to run for political office. The sound of cheers and desk-thumping filled Parliament.

However, Nellie was not there to enjoy the victory, for the McClungs had moved from Manitoba to Edmonton, Alberta, in December of 1914. In Alberta, however, Nellie had continued her work on behalf of women's suffrage everywhere. After the women's victory in Manitoba, the Manitoba Parliament sent a thank you telegram which read "from the women voters of Manitoba to Mrs McClung for the great service she has rendered her cause in Manitoba."

The pressure was now on the other provinces to give women the vote and the right to hold political office. In Saskatchewan and Alberta, women won both those rights only a few months later. Women in Quebec, however, had to wait until 1940, to vote and to hold office in their own province.

Women won the right to vote in federal elections in 1918.

## NEW DOORS TO OPEN

Nellie's eldest son, Jack, joined the army in 1915 and went off to Europe to fight in World War I. He spent three birthdays in the muddy trenches then returned to his family in 1919, forever haunted by the horrors of war.

In 1921, at the age of forty-eight, Nellie was elected as a member of the Alberta Legislature. As a member of Parliament, Nellie always voted for legislation that she felt would make Alberta a better place to live. She supported laws for old age pensions, for better working conditions in factories, for mothers' allowances, for a minimum wage, for easier divorces and for prohibition.

In the 1926 election she lost by sixty votes because she continued to support prohibition. Nellie shrugged off her defeat and became involved with the Persons Case along with her friend Emily Murphy and three other prominent Canadian women. The outcome was that Canadian women were finally persons in the eyes of the law and eligible to become Senators and to hold other important positions.

Nellie continued her writing career and also became the first woman member of the new Canadian Broadcasting Corporation's Board of Governors. In 1938 she was one of Canada's delegates to the League of Nations (now the United Nations) in Geneva, Switzerland.

Nellie and her husband Wes retired to live in British Columbia, and Nellie died in 1951 at age seventy-eight.

Once asked if she believed woman's place was in the home, Nellie replied, "Yes I do and so is father's—but not twenty-four hours a day for either of them. Woman's duty lies not only in rearing children but also in the world into which those children must some day enter."

Clearly, Nellie Mooney McClung did her duty as a woman and made Canada a better, kinder place to live.

Further Suggested Reading:

Benham, Mary Lile. *Nellie McClung*. Toronto: Fitzhenry & Whiteside, 1975.

McClung, Nellie L. *Clearing in the West*. Toronto: Thomas Allen, 1935.

McClung, Nellie L. *The Stream Runs Fast*. Toronto: Thomas Allen, 1945.

# WOMEN WIN POLITICAL EQUALITY

| | VOTING RIGHTS | RIGHT TO STAND FOR OFFICE |
|---|---|---|
| Manitoba | 28 January 1916 | 28 January 1916 |
| Saskatchewan | 14 March 1916 | 14 March 1916 |
| Alberta | 19 April 1916 | 19 April 1916 |
| British Columbia | 5 April 1917 | 5 April 1917 |
| Ontario | 12 April 1917 | 24 April 1919 |
| Nova Scotia | 26 April 1918 | 26 April 1918 |
| Dominion of Canada | | |
|   Relatives of members of the armed forces | 20 September 1917 | Made permanent by the Elections Act, 1920 |
|   All women | 24 May 1918 | |
| New Brunswick | 17 April 1919 | 9 March 1934 |
| Prince Edward Island | 3 May 1922 | 3 May 1922 |
| Newfoundland | 13 April 1925 | 13 April 1925 |
| Quebec | 25 April 1940 | 25 April 1940 |

# TIME LINE

Note: Modern place names are used

—————— **1600s** ——————

1602   Marie Jacquelin (de la Tour) born in Paris, France

1608   Samuel de Champlain begins the colony of New France in Quebec

1640   Marie Jacquelin arrives at Fort La Tour, New Brunswick, and marries Charles de la Tour

1645   Marie Jacquelin de la Tour defends and dies at Fort La Tour

1670   Hudson's Bay Company created

1678   Madeleine Jarret (Tarieu) is born in Quebec

1692   Madeleine Jarret (Tarieu) defends Fort Verchères

1697   Thanadelthur is born in Saskatchewan

—————— **1700s** ——————

1706   Madeleine Jarret marries Pierre-Thomas Tarieu

1713   Thanadelthur is captured by the Cree

1714   Thanadelthur arrives at York Factory, Manitoba

1717   Thanadelthur dies at York Factory

1722   Flora Macdonald is born in the Hebrides, Scotland

1736   Molly Brant born in the Mohawk Valley, New York, USA

1746   Flora Macdonald rescues "Bonnie Prince Charlie"

1747   Madeleine Jarret Tarieu dies in Quebec

1750   Flora Macdonald marries Allan Macdonald

1759   Molly Brant marries William Johnson

1774   Flora Macdonald and her family emigrate to North Carolina, USA

1775   Laura Ingersoll (Secord) is born in Massachusetts, USA

1776   The American Revolution begins

1777   Molly Brant's warning allows Joseph Brant to defeat the American Patriots at Oriskany, New York

       Molly Brant and her children are driven out of the Mohawk Valley by American Patriots

1778   Flora Macdonald moves to Windsor, Nova Scotia

1780   Flora Macdonald returns to Scotland

1781   American Patriots win the American Revolution

1790   Flora Macdonald dies in Scotland

1791   Quebec is divided into Upper and Lower Canada

1793   Anti-slavery laws are passed in Ontario

Laura Ingersoll (Secord) emigrates to Queenston, Ontario

1795 Molly Brant dies at Kingston, Ontario

1798 Laura Ingersoll marries James Secord

## —————— 1800s ——————

1800 Shawnadithit is born in Newfoundland

1812 War of 1812-1814 begins between Great Britain and the USA

Laura Ingersoll Secord's husband, James, is wounded in the Battle of Queenston Heights

1813 Laura Ingersoll Secord warns Lt FitzGibbon of an American attack

1820 Harriet Tubman (Davis) is born in Maryland, USA

1823 Shawnadithit is taken captive in Newfoundland

Mary Shadd (Cary) is born in Wilmington, Delaware, USA

1828 Shawnadithit teaches William Cormack about the Beothuk

1829 Shawnadithit dies in St. John's, Newfoundland

1831 Emily Jennings (Stowe) is born in Ontario

1835 Harriet Tubman (Davis) receives a head wound while helping another slave to escape

1841 Upper and Lower Canada are united as the Province of Canada

1849 Harriet Tubman (Davis) escapes to Pennsylvania, USA

1850 The Fugitive Slave Act is passed in United States of America

Harriet Tubman (Davis) makes her first of nineteen trips as a conductor on the Underground Railroad

1851 Harriet Tubman (Davis) moves to St. Catharines, Ontario, and begins guiding slaves to Ontario

Mary Shadd (Cary) moves to Windsor, Ontario, and opens a school

1853 Mary Shadd (Cary) begins *The Provincial Freeman*

1856 Mary Shadd marries Thomas Cary

Emily Jennings marries John Stowe

1857 *The Provincial Freeman* shuts down

1860 Laura Ingersoll Secord receives official recognition

1861 The American Civil War begins

Harriet Tubman (Davis) becomes a nurse in the Union Army

Mary Shadd Cary's husband dies; she becomes a recruiter for the American Union Army

Pauline Johnson is born on the Six Nations Reserve

1863  Harriet Tubman (Davis) leads the Combahee River Raid in South Carolina, USA

1865  The American Civil War ends

1866  Martha Munger (Black) is born in Chicago, Illinois, USA

1867  Confederation: The Dominion of Canada, made up of the provinces of Ontario, Quebec, New Brunswick and Nova Scotia, is formed

Dr Emily Jennings Stowe graduates from the New York Medical College for Women

1868  Laura Ingersoll Secord dies

Emily Ferguson (Murphy) is born

1870  Manitoba joins Confederation

Harriet Tubman marries Nelson Davis

1871  British Columbia joins Confederation

Emily Carr is born in Victoria, British Columbia

1873  Prince Edward Island joins Confederation

Nellie Mooney (McClung) is born

1874  Lucy Maud Montgomery is born in Prince Edward Island

1877  Dr Emily Jennings Stowe begins the Toronto Women's Suffrage Association in Ontario

1883  Mary Shadd Cary receives her law degree, Washington, DC, USA

Ontario Medical College for Women opens in Toronto, Ontario

1887  Emily Ferguson marries Arthur Murphy

1890  Maud Montgomery visits her father in Prince Albert, Saskatchewan

1892  Pauline Johnson gives her first public poetry recital

1893  Mary Shadd Cary dies in Washington, DC

Pauline Johnson begins her first concert tour

1894  Pauline Johnson travels to London, England

1895  Pauline Johnson's first book of poems, *White Wampum*, is published

1896  Nellie Mooney marries Wesley McClung in Manitoba

The Women's Suffrage Association puts on a Mock Parliament in Toronto, Ontario

1898  Martha Munger (Black) crosses the Chilkoot Pass into the Yukon Territory

1899  Emily Carr begins her art studies in England

## 1900s

1901    Emily Ferguson Murphy's first book, *Impressions of Janey Canuck Abroad*, is published

1903    Dr Emily Jennings Stowe dies in Ontario

1904    Martha Munger marries George Black

1905    Saskatchewan and Alberta join Confederation

1908    Maud Montgomery's first novel, *Anne of Green Gables*, is published

1909    Pauline Johnson ends her concert career

1910    Emily Carr studies the New Art in France

1911    Pauline Johnson's book, *Legends of Vancouver*, is published

        Maud Montgomery marries Ewan Macdonald

1913    Pauline Johnson dies in Vancouver, British Columbia

        Harriet Tubman Davis dies in Auburn, New York, USA

1914    World War I begins

        Nellie Mooney McClung plays the premier in the Women's Parliament, Manitoba

1916    Women win the right to vote and hold political office in Manitoba, Saskatchewan and Alberta

        Emily Ferguson Murphy becomes the first woman magistrate in the British Empire

1917    Women win the right to vote in British Columbia and Ontario

1918    World War I ends

        Women win the right to vote and hold political office in Nova Scotia

        Women win the right to vote in the Dominion of Canada

1919    Women win the right to vote in New Brunswick

1921    Nellie Mooney McClung is elected member of Parliament in the Alberta Legislature

1922    Women win the right to vote and hold political office in Prince Edward Island

1923    Maud Montgomery is the first Canadian woman to become a Fellow of the Royal Society of Arts, England

1925    Women win the right to vote and hold political office in Newfoundland

1927    Emily Carr's work is included in an exhibition of Canadian West Coast art

1929 Canadian women are, by law, declared to be persons

1933 Emily Ferguson Murphy dies

1935 Martha Munger Black is elected federal member of Parliament representing the Yukon Territory

Maud Montgomery is invested with the Order of the British Empire

1938 Nellie Mooney McClung is a Canadian delegate to the League of Nations

1939 World War II begins

1940 Women win the right to vote and hold political office in Quebec

1941 Emily Carr's first book, *Klee Wyck*, wins the Governor-General's Award for Literature

1942 Maud Montgomery dies in Ontario

1945 Emily Carr dies in Victoria, British Columbia

World War II ends

1949 Newfoundland joins Confederation

1951 Nellie Mooney McClung dies in British Columbia

1957 Martha Munger Black dies in the Yukon Territory

# INDEX

# PHOTOCREDITS

Page 10:Canadian Museum of Civilization 27007; 11:Joseph Bouchette, National Archives of Canada C47011; 12:"View of the Upper Falls of Saint John, New Brunswick," New Brunswick Museum; 15:"The Story of Acadia," Ganong Collection, New Brunswick Museum; 18:E. S. Curtis, Glenbow Archives NA1700-138; 20:NAC PA17947; 21:E. S. Curtis, Glenbow Archives NA1700-130; 22:E. S. Curtis, Glenbow Archives NA1700-20; 25:E. S. Curtis PAC C33530; 28:WGR Hind NAC C33685; 29:NAC C16952; 31:Mary Millicent Chaplin, NAC C885; 32:NAC C107626; 34:Canadian War Museum, #56-05-12-139, photos by William Kent; 39:"The Loyalists," Canada Post Corporation (#1028); 40:Sir Alexander Croke, NAC C3414; 41:James Peachey, NAC C2001; 41:W. H. Bartlett, NAC, C41662; 42:William James Topley, NAC PA10226; 48:E. S. Curtis, Glenbow Archives NA1700-34; 48:E. S. Curtis, Glenbow Archives NA1700-53; 49:E. S. Curtis, NAC C34803; 49:E. S. Curtis, NAC C33513; 51:James Peachey, NAC C1511; 54:George Heriot, NAC C12772; 55:James Peachey, NAC C2035; 56:James B. Dennis, NAC C41502; 57:NAC C1568; 59:NAC C228; 66:Henrietta Martha Hamilton, NAC C87698; 68:E. S. Curtis, NAC C38192; 68:E. S. Curtis, NAC C30229; 69:E. S. Curtis, NAC C19757; 70:J. P. Hawley, *The Beothuks or Red Indians*, Cambridge, at the University Press, 1915; 73:Regional Collection, UWO Library, London, Ontario; 76:Caroline Buchnall Estcourt, NAC C93963; 77:Robert Petley, NAC C115424; 78:Glenbow Archives, NA742-4; 82:NAC C29977; 87:Philip John Bainbrigge, NAC C11811; 88:William James, NAC PA126710; 89:From the National Film Board of Canada production, *Black Mother, Black Daughter*; 92:NAC C9480; 97:Yukon Archives, MacBride Collection 3954; 97:McCord Museum of Canadian History, Notman Photographic Archives, 28901-I; 98:Provincial Archives of Alberta, A-4985; 98:Glenbow Archives NA2674-17; 102:Provincial Archives of Ontario S898; 105:E. S. Curtis, Glenbow Archives NA1700-76; 105:E. S. Curtis, Glenbow Archives NA1700-35; 106:E. S. Curtis, NAC C20838; 108:E. S. Curtis, Glenbow Archives NA1700-55; 113:NAC C64915; 115:NAC 6816; 116:NAC 6817; 117:NAC 6647; 117:NAC 5392; 122:NAC PA10409; 122:NAC C63262; 123:NAC PA101109; 123:McCord Museum of Canadian History, Notman Photographic Archives 26,231-I; 125:Provincial Archives of Alberta, H. Pollard Collection P592; 131:Provincial Archives of British Columbia A-2037; 132:Provincial Archives of British Columbia PDP626; 134:*Big Raven*, Canada Post Corporation # 532; 137:Vancouver Art Gallery, Emily Carr Trust (42.3.1), Robert Keziere; 138:Vancouver Art Gallery, Emily Carr Trust (42.3.30), Jim Gorman; 141, 142, 143, 147,149:L. M. Montgomery Collections, University of Guelph Library Archival Collections and E. Stuart Macdonald Estate; 152:NAC C27674; 153:Glenbow Archives NA1029-27; 153:NAC C8891; 154:Vancouver Public Library #2023; 155:NAC C18734.

# ABOUT THE AUTHOR

SUSAN E MERRITT received a B.A. in English and a law degree from the University of Western Ontario. While at university, she won an English scholarship and an award for English composition and speech. As well as being a lawyer, Susan has researched and lectured widely upon the topic of women in history. Repeated requests from her audiences for a book on women in Canadian history have encouraged her to write *Her Story*. She lives in Ridgeway, Ontario, with her husband and two children.